Lemon Soap

K7
C6

First published by Lemon Soap 2004

Lemon Soap gratefully acknowledges the generous financial support
of the School of English, TCD.

ISBN 0-9547650-0-1

Cover design, text design and typesetting by Anú Design
Printed and bound by βetaprint, Dublin 17, Ireland

Lemon Soap
21 Westland Row
Oscar Wilde Centre
School of English
Trinity College Dublin
Dublin 2
REPUBLIC OF IRELAND

Lemonsoappress@hotmail.com

For information on the M. Phil. in Creative Writing
visit www.tcd.ie/OWC

Lemon Soap

Fiction and Poetry

from the

M Phil in Creative Writing

at the

Oscar Wilde Centre

School of English, Trinity College,

Dublin

One should absorb the colour of life...

Oscar Wilde,
The Picture of Dorian Gray, 1890

Nice smell these soaps have.

James Joyce,
Ulysses, **1922**

Staff

Managing Editor: *Sarah Binchy*

Editors: *Karen Bender*
             Mark Lawlor

Publicity Manager: *Catriona Mitchell*

Editorial Staff: *Dudley Cruse*
                     Jacqueline McCarrick

Acknowledgements

Thanks to Stephen Matterson, Brenda Brooks and the School of English, TCD; Gerald Dawe, Brendan Kennelly and Lilian Foley of the Oscar Wilde Centre; our lecturers, Jonathan Williams, Anne Devlin and Ian Duhig; and Laura Weldon of ReJoyce.

Contents

Foreword

They say (I can't remember who) that Judas writes the biography; so when I came to Dublin in January, I was determined that I wouldn't ask of the writers in the workshop: Who Are You? (too reminiscent of the fat caterpillar with the hookah who sits on a toadstool in *Alice*).

So we kept the book of biography firmly closed; theirs and mine, relegating it to History, so to speak. The resultant communications found their form in two aligned crafts: the poem and the short story.

The poets appear to have the most trouble keeping that thief History and its clamorous Dramatis Personae from making an entrance.

Noel Conneely's poem Lovesteps only finds the poet listening for the arrival of stockinged feet after the hardship years in Winter '56 (the cold war) and despite that fateful presence, the north, in Border Crossing. Alex Mavor makes his own valiant attempts to rise above the noise in his poems of sexual odyssey The Visionary and Marrakesh only to end up at the gates of Kilmainham in Last Kisses.

If a distrust of History's nightmare implies an allegiance to Joyce, the editors' choice of title, *Lemon Soap*, is a tribute to *Ulysses*. I have my own associations. A character in a play of mine leans close to someone and inhales the scent of lemon soap, because it banishes the smell of the pig lorry she's been travelling through the night in.

So I like to think of these voices as a trace of scent to raise the spirits but there's another meaning in the sound which is reminiscent of Gerry Dawe's poem Jazz Club, when his mother returns from an Ella concert — I'm sent, she says.

This is what it's like to sit in a room in a writers' workshop — it's as if the collected voices call out and reply to each other.

Ruth Greenberg's short story strikes the grief note in Louise at the loss of original innocence, I can still feel the vibration of that door shutting on the trembling apple tree, which draws Dudley Cruse's distinctive vocals in Lying In the Grass. This responding story really does raise your spirits, for it asserts the enduring presence of original innocence, to be found in the memory of the younger generation.

That these writers have kept time together is also obvious in Robert Monroe's echoing story of childhood friends in Lesson, about lost boys, one teaching the other to swim, while Peter Sheridan's contemporary lesson in looking is delivered by his artful persona in The Assistant in and around Dublin during the St Patrick's Day fair. If we're in the presence of life-saving friendships with the boys, it's the female voice that strikes a discordant note.

It takes Catriona Michell's story When Something Dear Goes Missing to remind us that Soap is no defence against reality and that lying in the bath is a little close to drowning in the bath.

Trudy Hayes's comic reclaiming of the single predatory female in One Night Stand begins the resistance; Jeannette Pascoe also embraces bad girl status in I Killed My Nanny On A Sunny Day, while Jacqueline McCarrick, the only female poet's voice, emerges from The Arch of Hysteria to answer her own call with a bluesy Medea.

More evidence that these women writers are passing through the same places is apparent from the influence of Louise Bourgeois's recent Dublin exhibition on Karen Bender's short story Double Entries. This story is a real narrative challenge and told with a wit as sharp as Bourgeois's needle; the writer doesn't want you to like her characters any more than she does.

Sarah Binchy's Gold Coat (impermeable to needles) is also a reading test, in its shifting boundaries between dreaming and remembering. As a husband skilfully separates his wife from her mother, we are alerted to the wisdom of keeping up that border between the erotic and ecstatic.

The arrangement of the material is so skilful in this collection that by the time I reached Mark Lawlor's poem Honey, I was thinking of Vishnu from the Mahabharata: it's the thought of honey that binds one to life. The poem has a curious echo of Cuchulain Comforted; except that where WB saw Gonne's eyes on the branches, Lawlor uses Christ's jacket to see off that troubled gaze. He returns to his true muse in his poem Hare. And Frances Byrnes's shyly comic tone starts the whole mating cycle off again as a woman contemplates an nonagenarian bridegroom in her short story 2 Proposals.

Any jazz singer will tell you, you are helped to find your voice through another person's singing. But you have to know your own cultural turf. Which just goes to show that you find out who you are and what you know through the sounds you make and not through your biography.

Anne Devlin
Writer Fellow
Trinity College, Dublin
5th May 2004

One Night Stand

TRUDY HAYES

I was at a gallery opening in the Blue Spot Gallery wearing my slinky black dress and spiky high heels trying to disguise my hunger as I guzzled every *vol au vent* in sight and I was just congratulating myself on my good luck when this short guy came up to me and stood before me, twitching nervously.

'Are you okay?' I asked him, taking in his studied attire – baggy trousers and a black linen jacket, a felt scarf wound around his neck. He had a meek face and nervous eyes and did not seem very confident.

'I'm a painter,' he explained. 'I was wondering would you do me the honour of letting me paint you some time.'

'Do you think you could capture my ethereal beauty?' I asked looking him up and down with some perplexity. He didn't look like a pervert anyway and he hadn't asked me to take off my clothes.

'I could make you immortal,' he said without a trace of irony. Modest fellow evidently, and yet I sensed he didn't have a massive ego.

I had had a painting framed by the gallery years ago and ever since I had been on their mailing list. For some reason they were under the delusion that I was of some consequence.

The paintings at this exhibition were dreadful. One painting appeared to portray various particles of the male anatomy. I could distinctly discern a flaccid penis and two testicles and it was not an edifying sight.

'The paintings are terrible, aren't they?' I said conversationally.

'They're mine, actually,' he said, looking hurt, and I instantly felt sorry, and protective of him. He had a bald patch which looked very tender and I had a momentary impulse to kiss it.

'Actually,' I said, 'They're terrible in a very interesting way. Sort of disturbing.'

He looked more gratified then and began to preen himself. I grabbed at a passing spinach canapé.

'They're about our ironic urge to give birth above an open grave,' he said, smiling at me.

'Our chronic what?' I asked.

'Oh, just a quote from Beckett,' he replied.

'Gloomy sort of a chap, wasn't he, old Beckett?' I said. 'A bit of a cod, really.'

He ignored this. I was trying to concentrate on the conversation while keeping a firm eye on the trays of food circulating around the room, determined to grab myself a hot crab canapé.

'You know you're very beautiful,' he said, gazing at me like a love-struck rabbit.

By no aesthetic standards was I beautiful but I made the best of myself and dressed with panache and style. I was looking particularly sexy in my little black number.

'I have very delicate nostrils,' I pointed out and he studied me gravely.

'Indeed,' he said. 'Perhaps I could sculpt you. I sometimes work in mixed media.'

I didn't fancy an image of me made in egg boxes but I smirked in a self-satisfied way. The thought of somebody wanting to paint me was very gratifying. Perhaps I didn't look like the back of a bus. He did though.

'It's a nice gallery,' I said, although I thought it was an architectural disaster – it was mostly made of glass, for fuck's sake, so there was no room to hang paintings.

I suddenly noticed a waiter. 'Oh la la,' I exclaimed.

'Oh, that's one of my favourite paintings, too' said my admirer, following my gaze.

Actually I was looking at the tray of edibles floating in my direction.

'Would you like a glass of wine?' he asked.

'Oh no,' I replied. 'I only drink champagne. I don't drink that cheap muck.'

I didn't let on that I'd already consumed about a gallon of plonk, which was even then rotting my innards.

A man with glasses wearing a swanky black jacket and fawn trousers came up to us but didn't deign to notice me. He looked extremely pompous and very self important.

He greeted my companion and shook his hand. 'Are you going to the *Irish Times* lecture tomorrow evening?' he enquired.

'What is it about?' asked my smitten admirer. 'Sort of Kundera-Havel territory?'

'No — more Salman Rushdie,' said my admirer, turning to me.

'This is...' he said and paused, 'I'm sorry, I don't know your name.'

'Serena,' I said, holding out my hand which he shook warmly. His swanky friend proferred his hand.

'Charmed,' he said, and I shook his hand which was like a limp lettuce leaf. I gave it a good shake, hoping to dislocate his shoulder. He backed away in alarm.

'Er,' he said, excusing himself. 'I'll see you later,' and he took his fascinating personality elsewhere.

'I'm Cedric,' said my admirer. 'We're all going for a bite after the show. I'd love you to come along.'

'Yes, I'd be delighted,' I replied, feeling pleased that I'd get some nosh. I was trying to write poetry myself which wasn't exactly a big earner and left me very little money for more basic necessities. The prospect of food could not be resisted.

However, the starvation rations I existed on meant that at least I'd a good figure.

I glanced around to see if there was anyone I knew. I spotted a few of the usual suspects – mostly minor celebrities and complete nonentities. Not out of the top drawer, don't you know. I wasn't in very exalted company. I noticed Joe Belton, an old sleazebag with the usual bimbo on his arm and Liam Maddigan, a tortured poet who wrote about dead sheep and Jim O' Toole who painted them. Peter O' Brien was there, looking resplendent in a blue suit. He ran a much posher gallery but it was rumoured that one of his clients was trying to kill him.

'Do you like that painting?' asked Cedric pointing to a painting which looked like a vagina with teeth. It had a red dot on it.

'Very menacing,' I replied, hoping it was the right thing to say, and he looked a little startled.

'It's a portrait of myself,' he said.

To be honest I was gobsmacked. Before I could make any comment we were joined by a couple of people I vaguely recognised, Melissa, a writer; her husband Jim, a journalist; John, a graphic designer and his wife, Lorna, a painter. Obviously they were friends of his, and he introduced me to them each in turn.

We all walked over to the Prospero Restaurant and I made myself comfortable and gazed around me. The restaurant was a bit like a bordello – all plush velvet seating and red velvet drapes hanging from the windows. An obsequious waiter scuttled over and proceeded to take our orders. Delighted with myself, I wriggled my toes in anticipation of a good feed.

The first thing that arrived over was a quail's egg which I decided not to tackle. I had ordered a rabbit dish for a starter and what arrived looked as though it wouldn't feed a rabbit. I guzzled it in one mouthful.

The main course appeared and I wired into my duck *à l'orange*.

'So fresh and yet so meaty,' I opined.

I snorkelled some more wine and the conversation began to drift around me. They were all talking about how materialistic people were these days and how individualistic society had become.

'There's no such thing as a democracy,' I piped up. 'All democracies are governed by powerful vested interests. Nobody is concerned about the marginalised in our society.'

I looked around me. They all looked fairly well-heeled and everybody was beautifully dressed. Lorna the painter was plump but attractive and wearing a dress which probably cost a fortune. Melissa was classically elegant in a tailored suit and fashionable high heels.

'You're just threatened by my intellect, dear,' said Lorna to her husband.

Lorna and Jim were starting to row and things were getting very het up. While they were all rowing I cleared their plates, snatching succulent pieces of meat and hoping they wouldn't notice.

'Oh you're so neurotic,' said Jim.

'I'm so erotic?' said Lorna.

I zoned out at this point but my admirer was determined to get to know me and told me about himself. 'They've all had a few too many,' he whispered in my ear. 'Don't mind them.' He told me his wife had kicked him out and he was living around the corner from her and his four children in a bedsit and I felt sorry for him. He really had very gentle eyes and a soft face and I saw he was a gentle soul. Suddenly I realized there was a more serious row going on around us.

'The only way you'll get your freedom is through the barrel of a gun,' said John shaking his fist. 'We had to bomb the British to the negotiating table by bombing the mainland.'

'The mainland?' Lorna grabbed her glass and emptied it over John's balding head.

Glasses were being pitched through the air as things got hot and heavy. Cedric leaned across and whispered in my ear, 'Will you come home tonight?' He looked at me with pleading eyes and I felt very sorry for him as I felt my heartstrings being tugged.

I suddenly felt like rescuing him and I decided to say yes just to get him out of the crocodile pit and he beamed at me, threw some money on the table and took me outside. Then I hadn't the heart to tell him that I hadn't really meant it and we took a taxi together to his dismal little bedsit. It was musky smelling and dingy looking, a sad little place. When he pulled me towards him for a kiss I decided to make him a present of my body.

He took off his clothes, naked and unerotic in the moonlit bedroom, his chicken legs sticking out of his boxer shorts, his arms flapping with excitement. I felt sorry for him and I took off my black dress and allowed him unhook my underwear. Shivering in the cold, I got into bed beside him and he made love to me clumsily. Afterwards I couldn't help it I was so hungry I ate him. He tasted absolutely delicious. Then I got dressed silently in the dark and sneaked into the kitchen. I opened the fridge and there were a few cold turkey sandwiches in it and I grabbed them and left, closing the door softly behind me.

Lesson

ROBERT MONROE

I was sitting on the sand, leaning against the stones, which were still kind of cool — but the sand was almost burning. This was the opposite of what my dad had taught me, that light things reflect the heat and dark ones absorb it. Maybe it's different for sand versus stones. The wind picked up and little darts of sand picked me in the face. I was squinting because of that and because of the sun.

Octavio came up to me. He was only wearing his cutoffs. Actually, they were Tommy's cutoffs — I saw his Alfa Romeo patch on the side.

'Are you hot?' Octavio asked.

I nodded.

'Why don't you swim?' he asked.

I shrugged my shoulders. 'Why don't you?' I said.

Octavio drew a line in the sand with his toe.

I kicked sand over part of it, from where I was sitting.

He stepped back and drew another line.

I kicked more over that one, reaching out with my foot.

He made another. I kicked but the wind blew it back, it was too far now. So I jumped up and stamped on his stupid line, smudging it with my feet. Octavio hopped back and made two more, really quick. I jumped and stamped on them and smudged them out; but he had already drawn two more and was halfway through the third, giggling. I charged right over the lines with my head down and decked him. We were on the sand, I was squeezing his waist and he was beating on my back. I started to pull his hair. He picked up sand and threw it in my face. It stung like hell in my eyes. I grabbed at them and he got away.

I was rubbing my eyes and it took a long time for enough water to come out to get the sand clear. The sunlight was very glary now and hurt. I really had to squint. The whole time, Octavio just stood there looking at me, not saying a damn thing, just staring at me with his big brown watchy eyes.

'You look like a goat,' I said.

He just stood there. I laughed. 'You look like a stupid idiot goat. Why don't you say something.'

He just looked at me a minute. Then he said, 'You smell like a goat.'

I jumped and ran at him and he took off. I chased him for a long way down the beach, as fast as we could. He was a fast runner. Finally I got an arm around his neck, we were still running, near the waves. He jammed on the brakes and started to go the other way, which looped me over his head like a scarf; my hands grabbed his ears. We were fighting for breath. We fell onto the wet sand, a wave washed up and over us.

When he felt the water Octavio started to flail at me with his arms and legs, and his elbow hit me in the face like a two-by-four. I held him closer — I didn't want him to get enough space to really hit me. I rolled towards the water and got an armlock around his neck from behind him, a half nelson. All of a sudden a wave washed in and lifted us up and then dropped us down on that steep under-water ledge where the sand drops away and the water sucks your feet down. We slid into the deep water and Octavio panicked. He thrashed like an electrocuted lizard in my face, grabbing my arm. But I kept hold around his neck: he couldn't swim — I had to save him. I started kicking like hell just trying to keep us both afloat. He was kicking too, but like a wild man, and he kneed me in the balls. It hurt but I had to keep on kicking. Finally, my feet found the bottom. Waves were coming in, and lifted us, but standing up straight I could keep our heads from getting washed over. I had my lock on him but he was thrashing, still pulling and kicking at me, a real danger.

'Stop it!' I yelled in his ear but he kept thrashing. I was losing strength.

Then I spoke softly. 'I'm not going to hurt you Octavio. Just stop moving and I'll show you how to do it.'

He went limp — not all at once, but piece by piece, like an animal or a fish dying on the grass. The wave washed his back up against my chest.

'Now put your feet down,' I said. His face tilted back as his leg stretched down along mine. When he felt his foot touch bottom his muscles relaxed and the human look came back into his eyes. He started to breathe more normal. I didn't let go of the half nelson though.

A wave came in and lifted us and he started to thrash and was about to yell but then we found the bottom again. A few more came in; he got better with each one. Pretty soon we were bobbing up and down like regular. His hair was drying, little waves of white powder on the brown, in front of my nose.

'Okay,' I said. 'I'm going to let you go.'

His shoulders tensed.

'It's easy,' I said. 'When a wave comes, just jump up towards the sky.'

I slid my arms down along his and picked up his hands. 'Also just move your hands in circles like this.' A wave came washing into us — I pushed off the bottom and circled his hands. I felt his muscles jump his arms up and down, jerky, like a squirrel. I slowed his hands down; his movements got smoother. We were standing again.

I let go of one hand. Octavio clenched up and looked around to me for help, but I just nodded at him.

'You can do it,' I said.

I let go of his other hand. A wave washed towards us; he looked terrified. But his arms started circling, quick. The wave came into us. His head stayed up. As it washed past, Octavio circled his arms more carefully, watching them, remembering himself now what his arms had remembered for him before.

He looked at me, and his dark eyes glimmered. Octavio grinned, the first time I'd ever seen him smile like that. He was on his own. Swimming free. Like me. The two of us like big free men. Well, I felt like we'd both earned it.

A swell came and he picked his feet up and started to move.

'Don't go too far out,' I said. I noticed the current had washed us down the beach a little bit.

We moved along, paddling parallel to the beach, not far from the shelf. By the time we got out, the skin on my shoulder was already getting red, and that night it really hurt. But it was okay. Octavio was a little burnt, but not too bad. He kept smiling, and I knew he was thinking of the waves.

~

The next day we put on sun tan lotion and did some more swimming. He was pretty brave about going further out. I got bored sometimes but it was okay. While he was practising I would look back over the water and up at our houses. I used to love to do that, to look back and see the McCormack's, then further up the hill to the back of our house, sometimes my mom or someone on the terrace, the window of my room. It was good now and the sun was bright but it was strange that the only movement now was a few repair crews and we had to worry about not being seen by the wrong people.

It took several hours for Octavio to learn the crawl, but he did. We had plenty of food, and magazines to read. For laughs, we turned on the religious guys on the radio and I would pretend to be a preacher, jestering to the birds from our terrace. Octavio knew the names of some of the constellations, in English and Spanish both, so at night, I learned those. We didn't look too far ahead.

One day I was sitting on the terrace rereading an interview with the manager of the Houston Oilers. It was very hot, we'd already been swimming, and I didn't feel like going back down the hill. We'd just eaten some canned beans, for about the millionth time. I realized how long it was since I'd left the hotel. There was no doubt that Jeanie would be worrying about where I'd gone and wondering if anything had happened to me. It certainly made me feel bad whenever she cried. I wished I could send a letter but — well, I might as well wish. And then I started to think about my mom, and what she might be thinking, if she were — but I didn't want to think too far along those lines. For several reasons. For one thing, if she wasn't there, and I got turned over to some adults I didn't know, then where would I be?

Octavio was sitting on the stone wall, eating peaches from a can, looking out over the water, his eyes narrow. I never knew what that boy might be thinking.

'Hey butt,' I said.

He looked at me.

'Do you know anyplace besides around here?'

'Sure,' he shrugged.

I told him some about Jeanie and Ralph, where they were living, how they had sort of taken care of me for a while until I got on my own feet a bit. He didn't say anything.

'Are you committed to staying here?' I asked him.

He poured out the peach juice onto a bush and tossed the empty can downhill. 'It's just a place,' he said. 'It's getting a little bit weird, with no grown-ups.'

'Well it's my house!' I said. 'So don't litter.'

'Sorry,' he said. 'But you're the one who wants to leave.'

He got up and went to my room. I heard him through the window, working with paper, probably on his map of the stars, which he was tracing from my World Book. I ran my finger over the edge of the seat cushion where I was sitting. Water had faded white patches into the yellow fabric, now that there was no roof, and a black squiggly line bubbled from one corner of it like the edge of a cloud. I didn't like it that everything was so crappy and unkept now. My mom would have been upset. She would have cleaned things up, I bet, if she were here. It seemed like if she were going to come back, though, she would have done it by now.

That night we discussed things. Octavio was pretty amenable either way. In the morning, we packed some cans and clothes and water bottles into the car. I watched our house as we pulled out of the driveway. One of the things about those days is you never knew if it was the last time you might see someplace. Wouldn't you know it, but my basketball court was still standing straight up!

'Hold it,' I said. I stopped the car, jumped out, ran to the garage, and grabbed my basketball. I shot a layup on the way out, and made it. I snatched the ball, and felt its smooth old panels. It was heavy in my hands, too soft to bounce well. I rolled it into the garage, where it settled against a rake. In the car, Octavio was watching me, but not honking or anything. I walked over and got in the driver's seat.

And then we left.

We drove northeast, through the hills around the city, speeding up whenever another car lingered alongside us. I'd put pillows on the seat, to look taller, and wore my Dad's shades, and a Padres cap. Octavio smoked. Once, some bone-head threw a rock at the side of the Mustang, but other than that, no major trouble. It's good to have a fast car.

Poems

NOEL CONNEELY

Border Crossing

Two soldiers board the coach,
birds' eyes dart
boots big as buckets.
White knuckles shine
on dull black guns,
a grim excitement
tightens their dogged jaws.
The first one feels a guitar soft case
for terror between frets.
A child shoots him a smile,
it glances off his armour plating.
This is Swanlinbar,
suspicion the legal tender.

Butcher's Apron

An old hand, he shows
the bacon how to keep
its best side out.

His hands are stained
with blessing.
He wipes them in his apron,
not so much like Pilate
as one who might answer
'it could have been me'
to 'who killed Cock Robin?'

At the counter, hungry shoppers
see the pink strips writhe
between yellow faced eggs
on greasy palms.

They shower him with praise,
but he needs no futile coin,
his soul's already winged.

Winter '56

That winter, the weather was so cold
we burned the old wooden clothes pegs.
With hope frayed as their collars,
we tied our faded shirts to the line.
We scratched drawings with our nails
on iced over bedroom windows.
Butter froze on the toast.
We taught ourselves not to cry
when tears came sharp as ice particles
on hollow cheeks.

LOVESTEPS

Each time the gate slams
it's the postman in boots
or the nosey meterman
with his little torch.

Jehovah's Witnesses,
a daring pair,
want to know if he has
a minute that lasts.

Is he aware of prayer
or has he found the Lord?
'Not at the moment,
didn't know he was lost.'

Love on the other hand
must come in stocking feet,
shut the gate so gently
he never hears.

Louise

RUTH GREENBERG

I would always wait for her outside the gate. Our parents had been friends even before we were born so I had known Louise for as long as I could remember but one day, standing in her kitchen in front of her mother, while she was getting ready upstairs, I felt awkward and did not know what to say. After that I stopped coming into the house and Louise never asked why.

We were good at talking for hours, non-stop chattering about stupid things. We would have screaming rows which would end in one of us turning and storming off, only to change our mind and swing back again, pinching the other one so hard they yelled out until we were both laughing. Sometimes we would listen intently, taking it in turn giving our opinions, but most days we would talk loudly over each other, not caring what was said, simply enjoying the sounds of our two voices mixed between us. But most importantly we shared silences. That was why we were friends.

It was November and as I waited for Louise on the other side of the fence that bordered her back garden I held on to the naked branch of her apple tree reaching over towards me. I would not be able to see Louise coming. Her fence and gate were easily six feet tall and made of planks nailed together with no breaks of light. But I could always hear her, banging the backdoor behind her and then crashing down the garden with her oversized boots. Her mother had once likened the tell-tale sounds to the toppling of the Berlin Wall and it did strike me, when she was out of sight, how much noise came from the tall, very slim girl that would the next moment be standing before me.

There she was, through the gate, out of breath, with her naturally ringletted hair carrying the aftershock of her journey down.

'Fuck, Peter! Mum will not get off my case. Give us a fag.'

We walked down the road, complaining about our parents, and then about school. Cutting through the park we reminisced about past times.

'Do you remember when we got that bottle of JD and came down here to drink it?'

'Yeah, and it started to rain.'

'Not just rain, it was pissing down.'

'Yeah.'

'And I pushed you and you went flying into a massive puddle but I was so lashed I lost my balance and fell in too.'

'But it didn't matter cos the rain was so heavy we were both already soaked through. We just lay there. We didn't get up for ages.'

'That was cool.'

We decided to head for the beach and see if anywhere would be open for ice creams. I was worried Louise would be cold as she had no coat, but she told me that for a boy I sounded remarkably like her mum. As we walked along I looked at her jumper sleeve and I could picture the arm inside, pale, long, and no thicker than the width of the bone itself. I wondered, as I often did, how it was she never felt the cold.

On the strand we found a vendor that was open, even though the place was deserted and the man served us our ice creams in gloves and a woolly hat. Louise ordered an extra large, double-coned whippy for herself and then jeered at me when I tried to get away with ordering a regular size. She told the vendor that I would have the same as her and I knew not to argue.

I ate my ice cream slowly, knowing that I would not want to finish it and worrying that Louise would make fun of me for being soft. When she crammed the last piece of her own cone into her mouth she turned to me. She reached out and took mine and finished it without saying a word, just smiling, her mouth open.

We reached the arcades but instead of going inside we turned down the concrete steps that led to the beach. Standing in the sand I watched the greenish rivulets of water that ran in lines toward the sea. The tide was far, far out. We made our way towards it, stopping only to pick up the odd clump of seaweed and lob it at the backs of each other's necks. The sand became damper and after a long while we found ourselves just a few feet from the water. I turned, looking towards the strand, but I could hardly make out the white shape of the vendor's van parked up along the sea front.

It was too cold to take our shoes off and paddle so we made do with running away from the breakers that chased us up the beach, trying to trip each other up as the waves nipped at our heels. Then we went searching for flat pebbles and when we had gathered a pile we stood together trying to skim the stones out across the grey water. The winter wind was strong, cutting jagged shapes into the surface of the sea that turned into sharp mouths, swallowing up our stones at first touch. Eventually our little pile was exhausted and I turned away from the sea, glad to be leaving the harsh exposure of the sand.

Except the sea turned with me.

I could see the strand, I could see the beach, but I could also see the water. I looked to Louise next to me. She was biting the chapped skin from her lower lip while her eyes darted back and forth in search of a path, a stretch of dry land through the waves. We stood on our diminishing island of sand watching the tide that had already crept past, encircling us, silent and unnoticed, and now licking away at the small area of ground left to us.

Louise moved first, walking to the edge of the circle.

"Come on, we'll wade it."

She stepped out into the water and it closed around the ankle of her boot. Another step and it had washed over the top. She winced. I ran over and plunged in beside her. The water was so cold that after the first sting everything went numb. It was almost as if my body was preparing itself, anaesthetising me against a far more momentous pain that waited somewhere beneath the colourless waves.

We were up to our thighs, and not even a third of the way across, when I felt the first rip of current. Louise let out a yelp and I grabbed for her hand, half expecting her to push me away, and was shocked when she clung to me tightly. We steadied ourselves against each other and then moved on, the water reaching our waists. I became aware of Louise moving away from me and I tried to strengthen my grip but her hand was slipping. She looked up at me and I felt my throat constrict with fear. She was crying. As I stepped towards her a wave hit from the side and I lost my footing. Our hands snapped apart and Louise disappeared, dragged through the skin of the sea. I was blind and gasping, the salt piercing my nose and throat. Another wave dashed against me and I felt every sense suffocating as the world around me swerved. I fell, clawing at nothing, struck my foot out, and hit sand, firmer and shallower than before. Suddenly I was standing at knee-depth in the water. I turned to face the sea and there was Louise, at a distance along the beach, crawling out of the foam. I ran to her and pulled her to her feet, holding her as she coughed and choked salty spit back into the water. When she was breathing regularly again I started to move her. Turning to make our way back to land I noticed our island had disappeared.

The silence that followed us home was not one that I had ever encountered before. Louise was shaking. I thought of putting my arms around her but I could not help noticing the way her wet jumper clung to her chest and I did not want to touch her. In the end I gave her my own drenched jacket to cover her up.

When we reached the lane that ran down behind her house she handed me back my coat. She turned and I watched her walk away. She reached her garden and as she entered I heard the gate bang shut. The apple tree shook with the force of its closing.

Poems

JACQUELINE McCARRICK

A Break for Sarah

She walk**S** through
biblical d**A**rkness
light as a b**R**ide,
her freckled f**A**ce
AbraH**a**m's moon.

White-haired **S**ister,
f**A**voured sibling,
her mouth is a da**R**k-fruit.
Element**A**l, prescient,
she gat**H**ers corn.

She hold**S** the tribe's
future in tawny h**A**nds,
the shephe**R**ds know her call,
vault at such **A**uthority.
she mot**H**ers rain.

In her apron **S**wings
gr**A**pes and apples,
always p**R**epared
for weddings, fe**A**sts,
droug**H**ts of his wine.

He remember**S** this

at the point of s**A**crifice:
'Sarah' b**R**eaks

in the light **A**ir.
She gat**H**ers her sons.

Note: A mesostic is a form most notably used by John Cage. He states: *"mesostics are written in the conventional way horizontally, but at the same time they follow a vertical rule, down the middle...I have something to do, a puzzle to solve...The situation is not linear. It is as though I am in a forest hunting for ideas."*

LUCIA

Fish-scales made me a sensation once in Paris,
Danced like Nijinsky, needed no rite of spring.
The language of maenads, lines not circles
Spoke it with hands straight, closed, Egyptian.

Short broken phrases, turned-in and flexed
Glistening fins deux fingres to ballet
With bare feet symmetry father loved,
Oh the words we made with the Duncan alphabet.

Strange these hands now cross me in the straits,
White-coiled and buckled round the wriggling fish,
Anna Livia as electric-shock rising to fingertips
Blue-veined, lulls me in the sky with diamonds.

Father, mother stand livid at the gate
To haul me away from the Jung man's needle,
Says the bloodline churns, turns black hysteria
She'll be here till midnight, Finnegans daughter.

Fish-scales made me a sensation once in Paris,
Silver-skulled sat in Ecole Normale, waited.
Fifty-years in Ivry, twentyforthly in one room
Slipped unbloomed from hands straight, closed, Egyptian.

Arch of Hysteria

I am the forgotten tragic heroine,
my name is this: hysteria.
I am pink and prostrate,
my mouth catches flies.

My veins hang loose,
wires hang off me,
I have been stitched up,
stitched up something rotten.

I am arched and I am waiting,
my bowed leg open,
I am waiting here for tears
to come and stop me laughing.

My hair has fallen out,
I'm a bald head sprouting
four short wires
tuning in to comedy.

My breasts stare at the ceiling,
my solar-plexus steels forward,
I am hoping for an Aeschylus
to come and write my story.

After Louise Bourgeois at IMMA 2004

Medea's Hands

These are the hands
wrung out your clothes,
cut and glass-dry
blood-lined and hard,

palms are the map
of the ancient world,
home is the spot
by a ringless finger.

I won the island
with spells and ointments,
a metacarpal success
found me early.

I have the touch
that is treacherous on you,
betrayal comes milk-flecked
with half-moons rising.

These are the hands
no mother could love
but as fists were adored
by the feckless rover,

On these wrists
I've been pondering pondering
I wouldn't be told
he'd soon fuck me over.

Do you remember
my dryness of fingers?
His land was so hot
I worked to the bone.

And my white nails
before they yellowed and clawed?
They were painter's hands
baked in the sun.

These are the hands
wrung out your neck,
blood-soaked your sister
with a stainless-steel cleaver,

fire-laced a white-knuckled
virgin and father
and still held a torch
for the handsome rover.

There is hell ten times
for the death-bellied mother.

The Assistant

PETER SHERIDAN

He reached over the table and seized the outstretched hand, shaking it. The seated man matched his smile and said:

'Pleased to meet you, Mr Ford.'

He sat back down at the table.

'Please Mr McAllister, Francis.'

Mr McAllister smiled anew, then turned his attention to the other person at the table.

'Willie – it's been a while since we ate together.'

'Sure Mac, I know. Even longer since we ate in here.'

The two older men looked around themselves in a way Francis could only describe as "wistful". McAllister nodded in Francis's direction:

'This one's a bit young to get the history of this place, Willie.'

'You started off waiting tables here or something?'

Willie looked down at his soup. McAllister smiled.

'Something like that, Francis.'

Francis toyed with the last of the paté and no one spoke for a while, the noise of cutlery, waiters and people eating rose up above them, filling the high ceiling. Francis looked up only when Willie and McAllister were deepening into a conversation he knew nothing about. He busied himself, eyeing the relative ease these diners around him showed in digesting cultured dishes and expensive-looking wine. The sun ran through a high window opposite them, forming a blue and yellowed beam from the smoke in the air.

He waited in the carpeted foyer as Willie bade McAllister goodbye on the steps outside the hotel. Willie returned through the revolving doors with an odd expression. He sauntered towards the red couch Francis was sitting on and stood over him for a few seconds longer than what Francis would consider "normal". He came to and looked Francis in the eyes.

'That could have gone better.'

Francis started:

'Why – what did he say?'

'Nothing. Nothing at all.'

Willie sat down beside him and emptied scraps of paper and a pen he was carrying in his pockets out on the low table in front of them. He was a few minutes at that, fingering and leafing and scribbling with Francis beside him heating up in his suit and trailing his left arm off the side of the couch. Willie rose and left most of the scraps on the table.

'Come on,' he said without looking at Francis.

They entered Kennedy's from Westland Row. Francis took an empty table and Willie eventually made it over with two Guinness.

'What did I tell you about impressions, Francis?'

'But you said I didn't make one.'

'Christ, Francis – to someone like McAllister no impression is a very very bad one. I mean it wasn't as if he didn't notice you sitting there. You shook his hand for Christ's sake. He made a choice to ignore you. People choose to ignore you, Francis – there's very little that gets past people – especially people like him.' He was red in the cheeks at this stage and tapped his beer mat twice.

'Listen. Forget it. Right? Drink up. I have to call into Marcus before four, so we've got a bit of time and I fancy a drink.'

Francis looked at him.

'It's all right Francis – they're on me.' He lit a smoke and side glanced the floor.

'Christ Almighty.'

He held the door open for Willie who exchanged a few words and a laugh with the barman. He hurried towards the doorway of traffic outside. They were past Pearse Station station when Francis stopped.

Willie faced him with eyebrows raised.

'I left the folder in Kennedy's.'

Willie said nothing and bade him get it with an odd wave of his hand. He watched Francis hop across the road before he himself ambled towards the Centra by the Church of St Andrews. He looked at the selection of croissants, Danishes and bagels with open eyes, finally picking up an apple and then a Fry's Chocolate Cream when he was standing in line at the counter. He ran his eyes over the headlines and started unwrapping the chocolate. The apple jutted out of his blazer pocket like a cloth cyst. He walked outside just as Francis returned. He rewrapped the chocolate and the two started back down Westland Row.

Willie waited at the lights gazing across Pearse Street towards the scaffolded Mahaffy's. Francis stood behind him palming his folder and studying the irregular patterns of sweat on Willie's brow. Willie arched his neck to face him.

'What are you doing back there – you're making me nervous.'

The lights changed and the two crossed together. They turned right at Mahaffy's and Willie made a left straight after, down a side street, and Francis followed.

Willie threw three squares of mushy Fry's at Francis as he disappeared through the red double doors leading from the waiting room to the offices inside. He opened the silver wrapping on his lap while eyeing the girl behind the desk. She did not oblige so he tarried as long as he deemed it safe before hanging his gaze on the silver rimmed clock on the wall opposite. The two of them were alone.

After two turns of the second hand he reached for his folder and began extracting his various papers and bundling them about on his lap. Nothing new drew his attention, yet he maintained interest in his task. He held out for as long as he could before putting them back. in. He left the folder on the chair beside him. As Marcus's office was on the side street no direct light came through the window, only a stale blue-grey which did little to hold his stare.

'Busy?' he asked the receptionist who was flipping pages. She paused and looked at him.

'Yes.'

He took it as a put-down and stared at his knees.

'Kind of,' she added.

He looked back up and smiled. She kind of reciprocated.

'So how's business for Marcus?'

'I wouldn't know,' she said, folding up whatever was in front of her.

'Whether he's busy or not he still wants the letter sent.'

He nodded.

'He's more pissed off now if that's anything to go by.'

He shuffled his weight from right ass cheek to left ass cheek.

'You working for him long?'

'Long enough.'

He looked at her blond ponytail, tighter than Willie's trousers. And that Ibiza tan.

'What time you off?'

'Probably past your bed time.'

She resumed flipping and he resumed scanning his knees for any changes.

Willie walked through the door with a kind of grin.

'There he is now.' He turned to the receptionist.

'Would you look at him.'

She smiled at Willie.

'Could you look at him?'

Willie found this hilarious and led Francis back outside to the tune of his hoarse laughing.

They swaddled back across Pearse Street, Francis with his hands in his pockets and Willie mollycoddling a rippled ice cream he picked up from a newsagents by Marcus's. Francis noted some of the more attractive Trinity students with side looks and half sighs.

'Oh it's grand to see young love blossom,' Willie said, shaping his ice cream with his tongue.

Francis looked at the ground and kept walking under both the sun and Westland Row railway bridge alike. They turned by the Davenport and on towards Merrion Square where the pre-Paddy's Day fun fair was in full swing. The Big Wheel was the first thing Francis saw, but as they squeezed in through the crowd his attention was ping-ponged from gaudy stall to angry parent to waltzer with a hectic, uneven rhythm. Willie tapped him on the head with a newspaper and pointed to the Big Wheel.

'Well?'

'You're joking?'

He finished off his cone and smiled, searching his pockets for coins:

'Car-ni-val!' he sang and gyrated towards the impressive wheel.

The attendant secured the bar to their carriage with a click and a hard tap then signalled the ride on. They left him waiting for the next carriage, gaining a slight height and Francis thanked God he could look above the faces of the parents and children and security guards. He looked at the car park of the Dáil, and noticed for the first time an archaic-looking obelisk surrounded by Nissan Primeras and sparse Gardaí slumped here and there. He turned to Willie who seemed lost in his own enjoyment. Francis looked back down to where the attendant was filling the next carriage with a young couple and their child – the child's candy floss waving about like a flag as the father bounced the child on his knee. Willie nudged him and he turned to an outstretched piece of chewing gum. Francis refused and Willie shrugged, loudly chewing his own piece as the wheel turned them another notch higher. Francis started to notice the stiff breeze as it flickered Willie's comb-over and he felt it play with his own hair. He sat on his folder so as to avoid any high-up mishaps.

He sat back down and saw Trinity College from above for the first time – he was amazed at its own world, secure from the rest of the city, like a weak castle. And Nassau Street, and the rooves of the Dáil, and glimpses of Stephen's Green and beyond it to the Grand Canal and Rathmines, the view in any direction running into a blur of houses only broken by occasional steeples, which stood like television aerials. He felt their carriage swaying in the breeze and gave the bolt which attached them to the ride's frame a once-over.

'Too late for that now, my friend,' said Willie grinning, 'we've, as you say, made our beds.'

Willie then surveyed the vista in a way Francis could only describe as "wistful". He turned to Francis and pointed vaguely in the direction of south:

'Would you look at that. No wonder those houses pay a fortune, you get this view from there. Without having to climb a fucking wheel.'

Francis gathered him to mean Dalkey Hill.

'Then compare it to that kip.' He gestured North.

Francis was still looking at Dalkey Hill though and the wheel brought them higher so he could see over it to Bray and then the Wicklow Mountains where the only piece of cloud in the sky was catching on them and coming apart, torn and wispy.

They remained at the top for around five minutes. Willie said nothing and started into the apple in his pocket with wistful bites. Francis was scanning the map of the rooftops flinging an imaginary superhero from one roof to the next, much like Spiderman.

'Listen, Francis.'

Francis turned to face him, swallowing apple.

'This little deal of ours, yeah?'

Francis nodded, feeling himself start to blush.

'Right – now I don't mind having you around, you know? I prefer the bit of company than none at all, you know? Honestly, I do.'

His comb-over ran this way and that above him.

'And you're free to use whatever you learn from me. You know that.

I've been doing this lark for a long time now, and I know its ropes. I know who's who, and I'll introduce you. Now here's the thing – I can only introduce you,' he paused, 'then you have to fill in the rest.'

Francis immediately answered:

'Yes – but I don't know what to do then – anytime I try to get on with them they take me the wrong way, or don't understand me, or put me down.'

'You have to relax, you see? You can't get it all by trying – you try too hard, and in the wrong directions. And when that doesn't work then you just go into yourself, do you get me?'

Francis could feel himself in full blush and welcomed the high blasts of wind that cooled his ears and cheeks.

'So what should I do?'

Willie grinned.

'Now here's the thing. Are you ready? *Nothing.* You do nothing. Not *your* kind of nothing, my friend – that's the wrong kind of nothing, do you see? You do my kind of nothing. It's more or less the same, except – I *look* like I'm doing something. You'll get it in time. You'll get the eyes – they're the important thing. The clincher in most business is the eyes, Francis. You can convince any man you're a fool or a Franciscan with these.'

He pointed cartoonishly to his eyes. Francis looked at them, and they flicked from Bugs Bunny to a real look of integrity. And then back to what Francis could only describe as "normal".

'Those there I call the "wise eyes". You can fool most with those. I've talked for hours about things I know *nothing* about, to people that honestly do, and they never guessed a thing because of these. They even leave thinking they've met a real expert. All because of these. They're more or less all I have. People don't set exams like in school, Francis, they gauge your body's language, and the main test of that is sweet Peter and Paul here." Again he pointed to his eyes.

Francis turned to the overview of his city again. The clouds had grown, tipping the outskirts of the city, and high gulls were scattering together in vague patterns. Willie finished his apple.

'Now of course – I wasn't born with them Francis, and there's a lot more to it than just putting on a look. You have to actually believe it sometimes, you know. But come here.' He stood up as much as he could in the small carriage and hurled the butt of his apple into the crowd below them, Francis followed it with his eyes and saw it burst apart at the feet of a security guard who started looking up and talking into his walkie-talkie. 'We'll take it every bit as it comes.'

Their carriage was shaking from Willie's throw, Francis held on to the side bar and felt under him for his folder as the Big Wheel turned once more and they started making their way back down.

I Killed My Nanny
on a Sunny Day

JEANNETTE PASCOE

Of course, it wasn't in cold blood. I was only five, and she didn't know how to play. She never liked me. She loved my little brother, the baby, the blond angel as she would call him, *un ángelito rubio*, to be exact. She didn't bother calling me anything and spoke of me simply as 'she' and 'her'. I was a pronoun of insignificance and I wonder now if she even knew how to pronounce my name.

My first memory of her is in the kitchen. I sat at the table closest to the kitchen TV eating a peanut butter and honey sandwich and watching *Mr Rogers' Neighborhood*. When she arrived at our house smelling of incense, I could see that the long thick fabric of a navy blue skirt was tight against her round butt, holding in her flesh. I mostly ignored her, perfectly entertained by Mr Rogers and his puppets. By the time my mother kissed me goodbye and left through the back door, I had finished one triangular slice of my sandwich and was full so I pushed away from the table and hopped off my chair.

'No!' she yelled at me for not finishing the other half of my sandwich and she made me sit back on the chair and finish it. It was a horrible injustice. I wasn't hungry and she made me eat. Not even Mr Rogers on the TV could take my mind off the food I had to finish. Looking at her under my wrinkled brow, I took a bite. The bread was dry and repulsive, and I consciously made my jaw chew up and down. That was it. I was full and couldn't chew any longer, not for her. I remember sitting there refusing to eat, but I'm not sure what happened after that or how I gained freedom from that table of torture. I vaguely remember my mother coming home, but that doesn't make sense. I would have to have been sitting there a very long time, unless my mother had forgotten something and came back to the house to fetch it.

My second memory is from the day she died. My parents left together in the old brown Camaro my dad used to own. Obsessively, I watched them leave. I stood on the couch that was positioned in front of our large front window with my feet falling into the pits of the flowered cushions. After pushing the curtains away I plastered my nose to the cold smooth glass, hands making prints on the shiny surface. I saw the car back out of the driveway from the side of the house and I thought that maybe they wouldn't see me so I waved as wildly as I could until I saw my dad smile really big and wave back, and I saw my mother crouch down so she could see out his window and wave as well, and they drove off. As I walked through the house I could see that my nanny was outside in the backyard with my baby brother, cooing over him and sipping tea on the porch. The house was too quiet inside, and through the window the watered lawn sparkled under the sun as the wind swayed the branches of the pine tree, making the needles fall delicately to the ground, so I went into the backyard to join them.

I wasn't any different than any other five year old. I wanted to play, so I ran around the yard one time for no particular reason except that I could. Then I ran to the swing, a new toy I had just recently learned to use on my own, and I swung as high as I could, thrusting my feet and shoulders as far forward and back as possible, gripping the chains with my hands so hard they began to pinch me. I swung even harder, enjoying the effort and the height and the wind in my hair. If I swung hard enough I could break off into the sky and fly away into the white fluffy clouds of Heaven.

My nanny began to yell at me. I was swinging too high. I shouldn't swing that high or I might fall. '*Tonta niña!*' she yelled, but I didn't know how to stop. I only knew how to swing, and I wasn't going to fall, but if I swung higher I thought I might go over the bar that held the two chains of my swing. Maybe she was afraid of me swinging over the bar. And I too became afraid that I would swing around in a huge circle, but I kept moving. She was getting angrier at me, stomping over, flailing her arm to get me on the ground, walking closer while holding my brother on her hip and I couldn't stop and she was getting too close. I was terrified of hitting them so as I swung towards the ground I tried to reach it with the toes of my shoes, but they barely touched and by trying to stretch them longer, I slid off the seat and my legs dragged on the ground, getting twisted into the dirt because I didn't let go of my grip on the chains. My knee and the palms of my hands were bleeding, but not badly, and she told me that I should have listened to her and it was time to go inside.

I didn't want to go inside, embittered by another form of her cruel injustice. I refused to obey her and even though my knee was sore, I ran from her towards the wisteria bush that grew large like a tree in the corner of our yard. She stomped closer, yelling at me to march towards the house, but again I refused and ran away. It was like a game my father and I would play when I would run away from him in the backyard and he would run after me until he caught me and flung me into his arms, tickling me as I squealed in laughter — except I didn't want her to reach me. I knew she couldn't catch me with her thick legs and pointy shoes. She was slow, and if I let her get too close she wouldn't attack me with tickles, she would grab my arm with her hand so tightly I would get red imprints on my flesh from her palm and she would pull me to the door. My agility was a power over her and it became fun to run past her out of her reach. 'If you don't go inside, I'm leaving!' It was a wonderful solution to the problem and I was glad to hear her say it. She placed my brother on a blanket in the shade, opened the gate into the driveway, and began walking away.

At first I didn't believe her. She was my nanny and wasn't supposed to leave us here. Would she walk the whole way? The drive to her apartment was never long but there were always houses with broken windows and loud music I never heard at home. I only thought about that for an instant. I was overcome by the joy of her departure and ran inside to the front window to wave her goodbye and she, glancing at the house from the sidewalk, saw me. But instead of continuing to walk down the street, she turned around, walked back to the driveway with her eyes towards me the entire time, making me feel trapped. Panicking, I jumped off the couch and ran through the kitchen. I made as much noise as I could with my Velcro sneakers as I stomped on the tile, pushed through the screen door to the yard and ran across the grass to stand behind the swing where I waited for her to turn the corner of the house and see me.

And when she did see me, she stopped and flung her arm up, pointing to the door with the firm non-negotiable position every child learns to fear without question and although I was afraid, I couldn't move. I didn't know what would follow that pointing finger of discipline. Never had I been so naughty as to ignore it and had always followed it, either to my room for a timeout, or to the bathroom to wash my mouth out with soap or, worst of all, to the nearest corner to stand with my nose touching the right angle of the walls, arms, legs and butt squirming for detachment like a bug whose wings are held by a drop of water, waiting for the eternity of five whole minutes to pass. But that day my heart was resolute and I was willing to rebel from the tyranny of her finger at all costs.

Her arm came down and the weight of fear lifted off my chain-gripping hands as she turned around and began walking away behind the corner from where she had appeared. I had won, I had won, but I couldn't let her leave without waving goodbye. That was wrong and unkind and what if something happened to her and I never waved goodbye. So again I ran inside and jumped onto the couch to flash her a quick wave, and immediately jumped off so she wouldn't get the wrong idea this time and would continue walking. I went into the yard once more and sat next to my brother who was amiably stuffing the corner of a plastic sandbox shovel into his mouth and then laughing at my game of peek-a-boo. I was glad to be the one in charge and felt fully capable of babysitting him until my mother came home. Then she would see that there was no reason to worry over me, that I was fine handling things myself, and that she wouldn't need our nanny's services any longer. But I was soon devastated when my nanny appeared around the corner instead of my mother. She must have seen me wave and come back. The stupid woman, I wasn't going to stay inside.

I stood up and walked backwards. She was silent this time and I knew I had unlocked a new level of her fury. She glared at me and walked closer, but instead of charging me like the bulls I saw in the cartoons on TV, she reached for my brother and walked into the house. I was suspicious of this tactic and uneasy at the fact that she could come back at any moment, but overall I was pleased. I began to sing and skip and cut lavender grape-like flower bundles off the wisteria bush to place behind my ears like a Greek god from one of my picture books.

My mother came home a few hours later to discover that I was still in the yard on my own. She asked where my nanny was, to which I triumphantly declared that she was inside. A few minutes later my mother appeared through the door with my nanny and my brother behind her. It was time to drive my nanny home and my mother wasn't smiling. She told me to get into the car and I did. I couldn't tell if she was mad at my nanny or me but no one said anything. I watched through the window as we drove past a group of people sitting on the hood of a dented car listening to music so loud it made our car vibrate. When we arrived at her apartment, my mother said goodbye to my nanny who got out of the car without looking at me. I waved anyway as she walked up the old wooden stairs out of view into her apartment.

The next day my mother sat next to me: we needed to talk about my nanny. I remembered with shame how I had refused to obey her and wondered if my mother still thought she could find honey if she kissed behind my ears. I watched her serious face, waiting for her to tell me what a bad little girl I was, but instead she placed a few new picture books on my lap and asked me if I knew what it meant when someone died. No, I did not, and she explained that it meant they were no longer on Earth with us and that they were in Heaven with

God, that my nanny had died and would no longer be my nanny anymore. It wasn't my fault, my mother told me, it was just her time to die, but I knew that I had been too naughty and felt guilty, but glad.

from Double Entries

KAREN BENDER

I have a friend born on every day of December. Actually, my wife tells me this. She's balancing my chequebook and noting all the deductions from last month.

'You can't have bought this many presents.'

'Have I bounced?'

'Not yet, but you're close, perilously close.' I can't manage to keep track of my purchases. I tuck the receipts in my pockets or even in my wallet but by the following day they're gone, inexplicably out of my possession. I can't retrieve even the memory of what I've gotten the day before. Oh, I can recall the CD that we're listening to on the stereo system and reconstitute perhaps half of the list of groceries that I bought at the market, but beyond that, the debits are erased from my memory and we have to call the bank or go online to track my balance. My wife has arranged it so that my account dips into hers if I'm overdrawn. She did this without my asking, before we were married. I'm grateful, but she says she did it for herself. It gives her peace of mind.

Obviously, my wife is orderly. She enjoys activities like scrubbing the side of the house free of mildew. Though only 33, she likes to talk about her pension and her plans for retirement. She's an engineer for the government and she thinks like an engineer, in units of structured association. She demands an explanation, and when I tell her she doesn't believe me. Statistically, it seems odd.

December 1st. My sister. She is a painter. A sculptor, too, I guess because she makes little figures that spring from her canvases. She likes medical oddities. I'd consider them one of her tropes because she frequently produces conjoined twins, etching details of their entwined organs into the paint, then enlarging the double heads or shared spine so that they leap into three dimensions. She uses a raku firing which leaves the sculptures with a blackened ashy surface. People think her work is disturbing. I find it funny. My wife is not so sure. She has speculated that my sister's work caused complications in her pregnancy but I think that is nonsense, superstition.

'I'm not thinking of superstitions,' my wife says abruptly. 'I'm thinking about toxins in the pigments she uses.'

'I don't know,' I say, 'anyway, my nephew is quite well now. A happily spoiled only child.'

My sister is also the fastest reader that I know. She can go through a 500-page book in an hour, an hour and a half, tops. And she knows what happened. You can quiz her on it. She read all of Proust in one weekend, for a date. She met a big collector at an opening and in order to impress him, she pretended that she knew what he was going on about when he mentioned Gilberte. They made a date for the following Monday, and after querying her friends about the character's provenance, she spent Saturday and Sunday locked in her apartment, scanning page after page of *Remembrance of Things Past*. When she went on the date, she was prepared to discuss all seven volumes with the guy but he didn't bring it up. Instead, he took her to a leather club called The Vault and wanted to lick her feet. She went home and had a nightmare and woke up and found the cat rubbing its coarse tongue across her ankle and called me to come over and keep her company.

The reading didn't help her there, but it did yield other insights. She was the one who told me that my best friend, 4th of December, was gay, this culled from a letter he sent me during his last year of high school. He had delivered me a note, a strangely ambiguous missive full of affection and fairly overt subtext (which I failed to see).

'Wait, wait, wait,' says my wife. 'I knew 12/4 was gay immediately.'

'You're more perceptive than I am,' I tell her. 'And it wasn't obvious then. And that wasn't the point. Can I continue?'

'Please.'

'My sister knew and it turned out she was right which caused some complications because the girl I was after was after *him*, and the only way I had a chance was to shake her from her obsession with December 4th.'

'And did you tell her?'

'No.'

'Good boy,' my wife says. 'I knew I married you for a reason.'

'We went on a date and I was trying to take her to the cemetery—'

'The cemetery?'

'My favourite romantic stop.' I can see my wife frown. She is learning new things about me. 'But it reminded her of December 4th and all she wanted to do was talk about him, so I took her home. She was the 3rd, but we didn't keep up. You'll notice that I didn't buy her a birthday gift.'

'That's a relief. Can I ask why the cemetery reminded her of December 4th?'

'December 4th had watched his father succumb to stomach cancer.'

'That's terrible.'

'Yes, but it created a kind of mystique around him, for everyone, not just me and 12/3. It was accepted that 12/4 had access to ideas and feelings we did not know existed. He was quite thin and had a funny walk but he was wise. He thought of answers to questions that never would have occurred to me.'

'For example?'

'For example, in school, we had a history professor who liked to employ unorthodox teaching methods. He advocated the importance of role-playing and when he assigned the students class presentations, 12/4 took up his methods. 12/4 was assigned to discuss the transition between the Carter and Reagan administrations and he chose the Iran hostage crisis as the embodiment of this period.'

'That sounds fair enough.'

'Sure. 12/4 asked the instructor if he'd participate in a role play and of course the teacher was flattered that his teaching methods had been taken on board by a pupil and he agreed. So 12/4 tied a blindfold around the teacher's eyes and knotted a scarf around his wrists and led him around the school while other members of 12/4's presentation group shouted carefully scripted obscenities and prodded him with a stick. They brought him out to the parking lot and led him weaving among the cars. It was a spectacle, particularly because the school windows faced out onto the tarmac and most of the students ran to the windows to watch. I was a year behind 12/4 so I was watching.'

'That's terrible,' says my wife, 'terribly cruel and dangerous and degrading.'

'Well the teacher didn't feel that way.'

'What? Was he crazy?'

'12/4 took off the blindfold and ordered one of the students to shine a bright flashlight in his face. He passed out 3x5 index cards to the class and each student yelled out the name of one of the hostages.'

'Jesus.'

'The teacher had a black eye but he was thrilled. The presentation had conveyed the emotions of the time, he noted in his evaluation. He felt that 12/4 got to the heart of the matter.'

'Hold on, there. What about the facts? Causation—'

'Causation is always a flawed—looking for a narrative in history is usually a mistake.'

'I can tell you must've done well in that class. What about revisionism? And why are we still calling him December 4th?'

'You asked me—'

'The bills, I forgot.' My wife pauses and checks off something in her double-lined accounting notebook. 'So who's 12/2?'

'December 2nd is my sister's gallery owner. She's also a big collector and she bought many pieces from my sister, though with a hefty discount because she was showing my sister's work. She was my employer in my very first job out of school.'

'Now I remember. I do remember a few things.'

'The job mostly consisted of looking at slides that artists sent in, occasionally filing them, more often trashing them or mailing them back if they'd included postage. The owner was an heiress and often discussed in the society pages, and she was secretly dating one of her artists. I knew, of course. It's always apparent if you're observant enough, and since she viewed me as her servant in the public world, I disappeared into the background and she'd talk freely about all the details of her intimate life in front of me. So she'd have me over to hang a painting or set up a table for the caterer when she was preparing an event for one of her artists and I'd learn a lot.

'She drove me out to her house in the Hamptons one time and that's where I noticed she had an awful lot of paintings by one of our artists, a handsome guy from Munich. She spent a lot of time looking at the paintings in absolute silence, then ordering me to change their positions, very slightly, a few inches to the left or right. I knew this artist had a girlfriend in Paris, but I also understood from the business' accounts that the gallery was paying for his loft space in New York. And I knew that the paintings in 12/2's Hamptons home were not listed in the gallery catalogues. The artist had a first-look contract with us, so all of his paintings would have been noted in the register even if the gallery didn't show them. Something was up.

'The positive thing was that the romance kept her mind off her own work. She was a terrible painter but a somewhat successful one: a gallery on Wooster showed her, probably thanks to her connections — I believe I mentioned her family owned a mass market baked goods outfit.'

'Good God, who cares?' says my wife. She is not a snob, my wife, and engineering keeps her mind free of the petty tyrannies of the social whirl.

'So, on the sly, she was taking the artist hunting in Scotland and travelling on safari in Africa and all I had to do was sit by the phone and write rejection letters.'

'Some career.'

'I didn't care. I wrote press releases and catalogue copy, so I was getting a little experience.'

'Well, that couldn't last.' My wife doesn't understand non-traditional employment. 'How did that end?'

'It was the Munich artist. I knew that the German was still seeing his Paris girlfriend while being a kept man in New York. I told my sister about it, but she advised me to keep quiet. People don't like it when you tell them about an unfaithful mate, I guess.

'So before their trip to Africa, the artist arranged with me for his girlfriend to come along, on the gallery's tab.'

'Wait a minute,' my wife says.

'I know, it sounds implausible, but the owner demanded that I accommodate any request from the artist. She'd gone as far as buying him his own plane when he started flying lessons, so I couldn't object when he had me book a flight for his French friend, from Paris to Nairobi, Nairobi to Mombasa. I figured that my boss would discover it when she looked at her credit card bill. But it happened that my boss left earlier than the German to go to the antique fair in Beziers and she didn't look at her bills before she left. I never did get all the details of the sleeping arrangements or how she found out but I suppose she finally did. She showed up in the gallery two weeks before her expected return, marched in when my sister and I were in the middle of a gallery-sponsored take-out from a bistro around the corner—skate *meunière* with some blanched green beans and potatoes and a half bottle of Sancerre.'

'And then you were fired?'

'Technically, it was gallery business. My sister had come to bring in slides of her work. She was moving away from *papier-mâché* to clay and kiln firing and she was eager to show me the results. I was happy to be able to take my older sister out, so to speak, to lunch. And after making sure that the cost wasn't coming out of her future sales, she was impressed when I told her it was on the house.'

'And you lost your job for a skate?'

'No! 12/2, the owner, bursts in and needless to say, we're very surprised to see her but she's so upset that she orders a leg of lamb from around the corner and sits down and tells us that she's left him. And we're about to get all the juicy details when she gets distracted by my sister's slides and loves them so much that she buys three pieces for herself on the spot. My sister had recently quit her job teaching at a pre-school for the children of celebrities, and she was beginning to worry about her living expenses so she was thrilled.

'But she wasn't relieved for very long, because 12/2 loved my sister's work so much that 12/2 switched from painting to sculpture as well and started imitating my sister's work and sent out her own slides and got into some really good galleries. People were mixing up the work.'

'I suppose they're not friends anymore,' my wife says shrewdly.

'No, of course not, but my sister had signed a contract with the gallery so she was linked to the owner for another year. But as luck would have it, she got married.'

'Your sister?'

'The owner.'

'What? Not the German.'

'The German.'

'I don't believe it. No, I take it back, this woman is awful.'

'It was lucky for us. The owner was so preoccupied with tracking down her husband and keeping an eye on him that she didn't have any spare time to keep the gallery open.'

'That wasn't so lucky for you. You were out of a job.'

'And I had to start paying for my own meals again. That was an adjustment, believe me. But it was probably time to move on. I wouldn't have met you if I stayed in that job.'

'I wouldn't have been interested if you stayed in that job.'

'Well, I met 12/5 at my next job and she knew your friends and that's how we met.'

'Remind me to get 12/5 a birthday present next year. And who's seventh?' my wife asks suddenly. 'You've got one through six.'

Poems

ALEX MAVOR

The Visionary

Picture this:
a butterfly in January,
stiff and angled
like a single propeller plane,
left out to gales, tipped onto nose and wing-point,
pinpointed on the edge of a black cobblestone,
stopped short of the crack that runs
rectangular in all directions, just as
words fit to sentences and later snag
on post-its, letters, lists.

Its wings are wedged open
not unlike the time the
Chaplain called in sick
and the cleaner decidedly, one hand to each,
pulled open the Cathedral's
oak-patterned doors,
or,
the inverse, the double doors in a restaurant,
when the hands-full waiter
has rounded his back to them, passed,
and the diners are left with
what happens in the kitchen
until the frame narrows
and the vision is gone.

I cannot impress upon you fully

the flight from Europe to Mexico,
the wing beats known by us
to be made by *Danaus Plexippus* once a year,
more precisely,
made once in the migrating year-long life of the Monarch butterfly
for reasons that weigh less than three to four grams.
Only can I tell you how,
cycling to meet you,
a bus pulled across my path.
I beat my palm flat against its side
stiff-necked and angling my head far left.
It left me behind, something
for passers-by to mention over dinner.

I would have mentioned it earlier but for the fact
I wanted to watch
the upset wingspan of your shoulders as
the black jumper was pulled upward
and note down in biro
another sure-fisted discovery
in the flight-pattern of the day,
seen in that first touch of night,
subtle as having slept then woken hand in hand,
distinct as the landing of
ten thousand butterflies in Dublin
come Spring.

ORANGES

are the last thing you bought me
before you moved on with the kids, car, CDs.

Orange.

The colour of boilersuits
at the prison you pass on the way to school,
and,
the loose fitting robes of holy men
we saw last summer performing the public cremations,
eleven foot pyres before the Ganges Temple.

Round like a fruit
centred in a fruit bowl,
like the unsold thriller, de-shelved, pulped,
cycled into a more romantic read.

Skin more dimpled than
the back of your hand as
you hold it under the light
in the guest bedroom
where you started sleeping last month,
claiming I was restless.

Turn off the lamp that drops its light, ripe,
on a golden watch that's kept the time these ten years,
placed by the sofa where you sit with re-found parents.
Check this orange is right.
Weigh its palmful of sweetness.
Buy it,
and if it proves too sickly
firm it
with the grip that
drags the dog, barking, by the neck
away from the neighbours' door.

The imitation-leather bound fruit,
breached,
juiced on your finger hooks that slip under skin with
whispers of 'Have you changed the bulb in the bathroom yet?'
The smell is unmistakably orange.

Tears wrapped in clingfilm after supper make up its flesh.
Clothes in a suitcase,
kids packed in the back of the car,
you in your family's arms,
an organic life,
these make up the
matter of an orange.

The seed of 'Things have got to change'
given root, turned to
pips spat out
and the rind of a bitter explanatory letter
to be tidied away from the kitchen table.

Too afraid to say to me,
to lift the phone,

orange, a fruit that does not show its bruises,
large
as a fist accelerating last thing at night,

orange
is what I think of you,
now that you left me
oranges.

Marrakesh

Start with the woman
on holiday on a walk through the city.
In the afternoon, give her limbs the length
of the white curtain-gap back in the hotel room where
he has his nap and maybe dreams about her

holding tight
to the guide book, a rubber brick
sunk to the bottom of the
bag made from the knowledge handed down and printed
in young yellow fingers weaving yellow reeds,
the bag bought this morning from among the
cross-stitched tit for tat negotiations of the market
where she now stands.

She wants another beautiful bag for her beautiful daughter.

But her fingers slip,
you made the brick too heavy or the bottom too deep,
her feet kick quick above her head
and she burbles to the vendor
'How much do I cost?'

At your signal, the tug at the hem of a sleeve,
the men's tongues start up their
flick, click, cluck and hiss.
Set in motion they make the move to pinch
the bareness of the backs of arms.

On stiff cotton sheets he lumbers onto his side
unable to hear her fish-cry from
cross-hatched streets sketched below
the surface of the window sill.

Close the curtains to the traffic.
Tighten the tap on its drip.
Sit squared away at the desk in the darkened room,
listen for a twig to snap.
Look for blood line left in the dust.
Arm out in front, pinkie and thumb divining the way
until

it comes into sight,
lopsided, off-centred, trailing a leg,
a woman flip-flopping down a street through a market in a
city spread out like the spit in her hair
with scratches down calves for streets,
face slapped with a foreign expression
knowing it must soon all be over,
just time to think
of the first holiday in sixteen years
she's taken alone with him, now the
doe-like young has grown bored with the old.

Open the door for her.
Usher her, bagless, into the bathroom.
Blow in his ear to wake him and
make him wonder what time it is.
It's the least you can do

since these are your words, your space,
the private place you visit every once in a while.
For surely no one else could describe
the curve of her cheek as she
insists to the mirror 'nothing happened',
and feel the repeated weight
of the water from the showerhead,
as she soaps herself with the door locked.

Puppets on strings
are beautiful things.
Your nicotine fingers
hook words clean out of my mouth.

Last Kisses

Planted by the woman made wife
in the candlelight of Kilmainham gaol,
full after the week's events,
an hour before the gunmen align
wondering who was given the blank.

X marks the spot
on the paper pinned to the
rise and fall of the not yet
dead man's chest;
and, from the heavens of our fourth floor flat
where I cuckoo out the window at midday,
X is the crossroads
where, down some rifle groove, I police and record
your movement into the Adult Book Store
as a sidle, practised at parties on other men's wives.

The last kiss ties a knot in the blindfold
making me think
of the time you're taking for milk and the paper,
of the morning spent lying on the floor
filling the album with colour photos of Dublin,
you, your fingers joking with the buttons on my jeans,
of how many people it takes to run a regime cleanly

versus how many to jumpstart a rising,
of the soil on the floor of a cell
so there's no need for a bucket in the corner,
and at the end of day, another sun put out,
the steam of his piss
which catches a man's cheeks in its hands
and takes a kiss before letting go.

Lying in the Grass

DUDLEY CRUSE

Your mother always lied, Richard says, rolling onto his side, now facing him. They are lying on their backs in the long grass. It is just new green, long new shoots that have sprung up after the rain. He is a metre at least away and his form can just be seen through the grass, broken up as it is, can see his movement more that anything as he rolls over to rest on his elbow his head held in his hand. Do you remember the time she told us that we would grow horns if we ate while lying down in bed?

I never believed that.

You did too! Richard says, sitting up indignant. You shouted at me the next day when we were lying around watching TV and I was eating my rusk lying down on the couch, you told me I would grow horns from my head.

And.

And I told you that I wasn't lying in bed so I would be fine. He lies down again on his back, his hands overlapping behind his head, holding his head in his hands, cupped in his hands, the left over the right. Didn't your brother tell us that he could eat in bed because he was older and only children grew horns?

I don't remember.

We caught him in bed with an apple. And he said he could. There is a pause; silence, and birds can be heard in the trees nearby, singing in the sun that has emerged from behind the single cloud stuck in the sky. There is no wind there is only sky and sun and the itchy green of the grass around them. The humidity of the grass that is alive and still growing. The ground that is a little damp from the rain last night, that will take all day to dry out and.

He is aware of his own breathing and of the soil under his hands that are behind his head, he can feel the small grains digging into his skin that will leave red marks, little indentations, dimples in the skin and will fade again as the skin lifts out. He can feel the hair on his head against the palm of his right hand, can feel it slide when he moves his head from side to side to scratch. So much grass around him makes him itch, makes his scalp itch and crawl a little, even though it is not really touching him. He takes a deep breath to fill his lungs, as much as he can, and holds and then tries to suck in more until it is painful and then and then slowly lets it out, dribbling out, through pursed lips.

Do you remember, Richard says, when we were at the sea and we found your brother upstairs in the lounge with his girlfriend, what was her name?

Doris.

Don't be stupid man. What was her name?

Jennifer or something. I forget.

Right. Jennifer. And we knew he was going upstairs with her and we ran outside, climbed that rock, the rock that sat next to the window, and tried to spy on them.

We giggled too much though.

Yes. Ha. It was funny though. What he looked like when he saw us, him lying prone on the couch and she half on half off him, her dress riding up. He was so red.

He shouted and jumped up and she fell onto the floor and he ran out the door to come find us outside and beat us.

I don't think he would have hit us. He just wanted to chase us because he was angry. I don't think he would have known what to do with us if he had caught us.

Jesus I was scared though. He laughs softly to himself and the other can't help laughing too, just a little. He did look like a bit of a raging red monster his face all red, he says, specially with the red hair and everything.

And the red face and I swear his eyes.

Now you're just imagining things.

Maybe, but that's how I remember it. He can hear the other boy breathing nearby in the grass, but he cannot see him because he is looking at the sky and watching the flocks of birds fly across him. He has to move his hands from out behind his head. They were beginning to hurt. Across the knuckles and along the bones and tendons of his left hand pressed into the ground by the weight of his head. Your dad, Richard says, didn't know whether to be angry with us or laugh.

But Michael wouldn't let him let us get away with it, kept telling my dad to do something about it.

He did whine sometimes.

Still does every now and again. I can see him jumping up and down demanding that he punish us, like he was holding on a full bladder and thought he was going to give way any second, jumping up and down.

He remembers. They were 12. It had been on the holiday they had taken to the beach. The first time they had gone down to the coast in four or five years. He had brought Richard along as his friend. His brother had brought Jennifer, though she had slept in the girls' room with his two sisters. It had been on a hot afternoon, when they had all gone upstairs to lie down and attempt to escape the humidity and heat, that they had found his brother and the girl on the couch. He remembers then that holiday lying on the bed sweating at night, his back sticking to the sheet, his neck damp against the pillow and the windows left open to allow the air in. Letting in the light from the street throws patterns on the ceiling that he watches, unable to sleep.

He can still hear the whirr of the small standing fan, clacking when it reaches the end of its arc and then swings back again bringing the moving air pouring over him for a few seconds before it moves on. He can hear the others breathing in the room, his brother and Richard, he can hear that they are asleep, that they cannot feel the sweat coating their bodies and smell the bodies slowly roasting. Feeling like a lobster thrown into the pot, too weak to scream really, feeling the heat in your armpits underneath your fingernails, feel it building even behind your eyelids when you close them.

The girls got the better room with the ceiling fan and more than one window. Lying there in the heat he imagines his brother waking up at an appointed time; getting up quietly, unaware that his brother is awake, sneaking down the creaking stairs, tip-toeing only in his pyjama shorts. To meet her in the driveway still in her nightie. It flutters a little in the breeze blowing off the land out to sea, taking the air with it, white thin cotton that does not hide her form. He takes her hand and they turn to walk down the steep drive and then through the garden across the street where the dog behind the fence barks at them and they begin to run, giggling a little, holding hands.

Walking they get to the beach, the first step onto the soft coarse sand, your toes sinking into it, sand flicking up behind them as they run out onto the beach and stand then looking at the sea in the moonlight; can hear the throb and beat of it against the shore, can feel the sound impact in their chests in their brains, and the wind against their skin. Right at that point there, at that time, they will love each other always, even if they themselves don't know it. Are too young. He imagines them holding hands for minutes, for ages and he feels jealous, feels guilty for intruding.

Lying in the grass now he wonders where Jennifer is, what she is doing. He works out quickly that she would be 21 or 22, is probably still at university or maybe even finished.

What're you thinking? Richard asks him from the grass a meter or so away.

He smiles to himself and wonders how long they have been lying in silence, how far the sun has moved. The air is relaxing, the sun is in his face now shining directly into his eyes, the sky is clear and immense towering over them. He says, I was just wondering where Jennifer is now, where she went.

What? After your brother broke her heart?

He sits up. He sits up, bends his legs at the knees, holds them with his arms, his elbows at his knees, a knee in each elbow with his forearms overlapping. Each hand gripping the other arm, holding him in place with his head turned away looking over the grass down towards the mango trees, purple unripe fruit hanging, down towards the hill beyond them and the hill beyond that and the town he can see spreading there up the sides of the round hills. His town.

Ja. Shame. I guess it doesn't really matter. I mean she doesn't mean anything to me obviously, but I didn't see her after they left high school. And it's weird when anyone just disappears like that.

Don't worry there. I'm not going to disappear from your life.

He looks over quickly at Richard who is also sitting now and can be seen, emerged from the grasses for the first time, his dark hair short and rubbed up the back by the ground. Richard is grinning at him and he picks up a small stone to throw at him and says, Don't be a moron. I was just talking, don't have to make fun. So saying he stands up. Come we had better go, your mom will be looking for us.

When Something Dear Goes Missing

CATRIONA MITCHELL

Although it seemed like giving up, Anita decided to accept the offer. Liz was pregnant with twins and would shortly require larger premises. Anita had long found herself rattling around the Ravenscourt Park house, which was at once too empty, and too full of ghosts, for her to be at peace there. The cut, Anita told herself, would be painful but clean, like a surgical operation. The first of January was the date they settled upon. After Anita had cried hot tears into cold bathwater, blown a collection of candles out at midnight to herald the new year, and crawled in the dark to a final, chilly night in her four-poster bed, the two women swapped addresses.

Anita's new home was only two blocks from the old one. It meant that she could visit her garden frequently. This, at least, was a comfort. The garden would always be Anita's, even when the twins were playing hide and seek in its shadows, mashing its blossoms into a perfumed pulp, disturbing the perfect sculpture of the flower beds with their little Wellington boots. Everything there Anita had planted herself, digging the frozen ground until her fingers bled. Urgent for new life. All of the plants in that garden would blossom white, in their turn. Liz didn't know that yet.

Anita's new house was a three-storey terrace, slim and tall like a domino. It looked austere from the outside, with its bare brick façade and peeling front door against which the street litter accumulated like insects on flypaper. The first thing Anita did even before unpacking the tea chests, was go to the nursery and buy window boxes full of geraniums. Scarlet, cerise, pale pink. Colours this time; she was beginning anew. But they were vandalised, the pots broken into jagged terracotta shards and their earth spilled across the pavement, the first night. She knew it was the gang who hung around the tube station, its entrance deserted and gaping like a dark mouth, forbidding as the expression in the young men's eyes. Anita was afraid of the simultaneous boredom and violence that emanated from the youths, their clamorous cravings for something to numb or stimulate, something to create or more likely, destroy. She averted her gaze when they passed the house. She didn't complain about the geraniums.

Inside, the house provided a rich shelter. Double-glazing shut out the gang's scuffles, the scraping-metal noise of the trains, the multi-cultural singsong of the King's Road. Anita fitted an iron bar across the back of the front door and grew to feel safe, at home, in the pint-sized rooms. She kept the shutters closed on the ground floor, had Sainsbury's deliver her essentials and arranged for her cleaner to come once a week. She sat in her frayed dressing gown in her office, attempting to write often until twilight. During her breaks she'd wander from floor to floor, her hand clasped around a handmade pottery mug of sugared tea. She took in the details of her home with a grunt which, though gruff, was a signal of satisfaction.

The house had retained its Victorian flavour: the original floor-boards were polished, the ceiling-roses and miniature tiled fireplaces preserved. The rooms were rich and sumptuous like the walls of a jewellery box, each painted in a bold colour — burnt umber, emerald, azure, petrol blue. The kitchen could only accommodate one chef at a time, but Anita doubted that would prove a problem. She ate little; she seldom cooked for herself and never for other people. She had always considered herself to be of a cerebral rather than a sensual nature. Rare and antique books were her passion. She had a man come in to mount shelves wherever they'd fit – in the bedrooms, on the stairway – and unpacked her collections with a rare joy. To her own novels she gave the most prominent place in the entrance hall, by the mahogany coat stand: a place where visitors, should they find themselves in her home, would be sure to notice them. On the richly coloured walls she hung the treasures she and Leonard had collected on their travels: an embroidered Peruvian wedding-blanket, a coarse, hand-woven kilim, a flat piece of eucalyptus bark depicting the Aboriginal dreamtime.

The fact that the cat seemed to like the house, she took to be a good sign.

The bathroom on the top floor was her favourite. Incongruously, it was the room with the most generous proportions, and the tub sat majestic by the window like a lion on golden claws. Anita spent one evening after another there, mixing a cocktail of essential oils that made her drowsy or lively or both, boiling several kettles in advance, lining them up on the floor by the tub so she could replenish the hot water at will after the tap water had run cold.

The tall window by the tub looked out over the London rooves: tiled and slate grey, slippery with rain. Only the roof directly behind her house was different. It was made of glass, like a greenhouse, and glowed warm with a yellow light after dusk. It intrigued her, and she gazed at it from her aqueous vantage point. A painter was at work below in the glassed-in space. He was always there: like her, he never seemed to go out. She could never make out what he was working on — her eyesight wasn't good enough – but she could make out the triangle of his easel, the flash of his balding head, a vague impression of his movements and shadows.

Most of the time, steeping in the steam and the heat, Anita was thinking of Leonard, recreating the experience of him, feeling the essence of him course through her. She panicked when she thought he might come back to the old house to find her gone. She had to calm herself with precise, rational thought, talking herself through it as if to a child. Liz would direct him here. He would come to this house, and find her in the bath, fragrant, waiting for him, gently poised. Like a limpid queen. Or Marat.

As distraction from her worry, and to pay the bills that were shoved with regularity under her peeling front door by a whistling postman, Anita was writing a novel. It was an attempt at something light: a romance. She would give it a happy ending. When the first three chapters were done, she decided to send them to her agent. It was a long time since she'd been out of the house. The post office was not far, on the corner of her street. She went in a long fur coat she'd bought in a treasure trove of designer and vintage clothing, near Sloane Square. Underneath it, she wore her pyjamas. No one would notice. It must have been social welfare day. The queue was long, and didn't seem to be moving. An advertisement over the counter read in almost illegible scrawl, on a scrap of brown cardboard: 'Post office assistant wanted. Must be over 65'. Anita wondered if this specification was to discourage the disenfranchised youths in the queue before her from applying.

Her agent rang three nights later. She didn't like the book; she found it depressing, a mish-mash of bitterness and despair. *People don't want to read your dirty laundry.* Anita was in the bath when she received the call. She had thought at the last minute to bring the cordless phone up with her, in case Liz called. Or Leonard. *Lord knows you've been through troubled times. But try to write something a bit more* up *for your readers, won't you darling?*

She stayed in, writing in spurts but more often staring at the walls, going out only to walk through Ravenscourt Park to Liz's, for a cup of decaf and to visit the garden. Liz was busy giving cello lessons when she wasn't preparing for motherhood; she didn't have time to visit in return. For all her pride in its detail, and despite the fresh, careful start she'd hoped to make, Anita started to neglect her house. Half-eaten sandwiches lurked forgotten on the windowsills. The kitchen table became so laden with newspaper cuttings, postcards, coins, CDs out of their cases, pairs of broken spectacles, that it was near impossible to find space for a plate or a glass or a knife and fork. In the bathroom, tubs of cold cream were left with their lids off, their sticky contents gathering cat hair. Half-empty packets of HRT tablets lay among the furballs on the floor.

Kathy, the wide, gold-toothed Grenadian who had been cleaning for Anita even before Leonard's disappearance, tut-tutted to herself when she saw the state of this place. However, it was in her nature to be optimistic, even in the face of opposition. Pretty soon you'd believe your own deceptions — that was her philosophy. 'You're much better since you got here, Mrs Hoff,' she encouraged her employer, 'You're making more of an effort with yourself, isn't it?'

Kathy began to bring Grenadian specialties from her kitchen to the house; she couldn't bear to see Anita so anaemic and under-weight. She heated pancakes made with cornflour and stuffed with spiced lentils in the microwave. She left a stack of them in the freezer, each one folded into quarters and wrapped in clingfilm. The food was greasy and fragrant. It sat undigested in Anita's stomach for hours after she'd eaten it. She was never hungry but it felt reassuring there, like an anchor.

On a Friday afternoon, just after Kathy had departed, leaving the floorboards damp and lemon scented, the doorbell rang. A police-man was standing on the stoop. 'Good afternoon, Madam,' he said awkwardly, avoiding Anita's eye, shuffling from one foot to another. Anita realized she was in her dressing gown and hadn't brushed her hair. She attempted to pat it down with one hand.

'Yes?'

'Madam,' he said again, 'I'm afraid it's my duty to report...'

A delayed response, his presence now hit her like a blow to the head. This was it. This was the day it would happen, this day, though a few minutes ago she hadn't known. It surprised her that her instincts had provided no fore-warning. She swooned and reached for the doorframe to steady her, aware of the blood draining from her face.

'Madam? Is everything all right?'

With the towelling sleeve of her dressing gown, she dabbed at the perspiration – liquid panic — that had broken out on her brow. The cool winter air, though laden with traffic fumes, revived her.

'Perhaps you'd better come inside,' she whispered.

'If it's all the same to you, madam, I'd rather not. This won't take a moment. Whenever you're ready....'

Anita nodded her assent.

'You see, madam, I've had a call from one of your neighbours, a Mr Richmond from Blythe Road.'

'Blythe Road?'

'Yes, madam. It's the one behind yours.'

'Is it?'

'Yes, madam.'

She nodded. This was interminable. Why was he taking so long? She needed the blade to fall swift and clean, now that her fate was decided, like a guillotine. *La veuve.* How cruel language could be.

'Leonard?' It came out as a whisper, a whimper.

'Leonard? No, I believe his first name is Howard, ma'am. How can I put this. It seems you've been a bit of a – how shall I say it – well, to use Mr Richmond's own words, a Peeping Tom.'

'A what?'

'He seems to think you observe him rather often from a big window on your top floor.' A blush of purple crept over the policeman's neck as he spoke. Relief flooded through her. It wasn't going to be today after all. She started to laugh, slowly at first but more and more manically, relieved and heartbroken, then she was crying too, without being able to stop. She wiped at the stream of tears with the edge of her hand. Her lungs hurt as if they'd been torn.

'Madam?' The policeman was beginning to lose patience. 'If you don't mind me saying so, this is a serious matter?'

'I'm sorry. It's just…you see….'

'Although he doesn't object in principle to being watched, Mr Richmond felt it necessary to mention your habits. You see, several paintings went missing last night from Mr Richmond's studio. He is quite distraught. You know how these artists get. He was hoping you might have noticed something.'

'Oh. I see.' Anita was silent a long while, leaning against the door frame. When she spoke again she selected her words with care. 'Please, tell this to your Mr Richmond. I have no idea who marauded his studio, and I'm sorry for his loss. I know what it is when something dear goes missing. But tell him to forget those paintings. Tell him life is drained of all merit, when all that matters becomes that which isn't....' She wanted to go on but her tongue stopped dead in her mouth, something thick and lifeless that no longer belonged to her. She put her hands over her eyes.

The policeman was waiting for her to finish. She took a deep breath, and when she managed to speak again, her voice was feeble as if her own words were sapping her of all her strength. 'Life is drained of all merit when all that counts is that which is not there.'

Anita retreated backwards into her hallway then, leaving the policeman on the first step, looking after her, bemused. She walked to the kitchen, her breathing irregular, her heart palpitating. With a trembling hand she turned the tap and began to fill the kettle for a bath.

Gold Coat

SARAH BINCHY

I am wearing a gold coat with brass buttons that snap together. My mother hunkers down to fasten my coat and as she does so we hear low, mournful flute music. Each button is sounding a different note.

My coat is playing 'Danny Boy'.

Somehow, this is not remarkable.

We are on the Marine Road and the sea looms up to us. Now we are in a shop I thought had closed down. I am trailing behind my mother. We used to buy my school uniforms here. I remember it as dark with rolls of dusty material stacked like logs behind the counter, but now the windows are bright and the clothes are magnificent.

I linger over something in frayed pink tweed with creamy chiffon beneath.

A man, it is my husband, but this is not strange, appears at my shoulder to remind me he thinks classic cuts suit me best, and vanishes.

Now my mother is ahead again. I struggle to catch her up as she strides on, calm, aloof, and pauses that way she does, grinding a kernel of disdain in her fingertips as she feels the stuff of a dress. 'Will it always be that you lead and I follow?' I ask. The words come out bitterly but that is not how I meant them at all.

We are visiting my mother in a house near the sea.

This is where she has been living all the time!

We walk up a flight of grey stone steps. My husband is a little shy, and hides behind me.

She meets us at the door. She does not speak but reaches out a hand and there is apology in her eyes. We can see right through the house to back windows on to the lashing sea, and her wide airy living-room, cream carpets and a piano and books and papers lying around. If my mother liked the piano why did I not know? She's happy here, I think. Then I look again at her face, which is not her face at all, but somebody else's, a thinner, older woman's face from a painting, grey hair in a fringe and three sharp stripes on each cheek, as though somebody has carved them with a chisel. She is smiling, but wanly, with pain. This is not my mother's face.

She phones me. She is in Holyhead. No, she is on the mailboat. She is in the middle of the sea. She is nearly in Dun Laoghaire. She is crying, or else the gulls are. She says, look out your window. There is the boat moving steadily across the bay, about ten minutes from the harbour.

It's all true. I can see her. She has all the letters and diaries she ever wrote for me and about me, clutched in her hand. 'Just come and get me, hurry up,' she says. 'Get in your car and come and get me, for the love of God.'

I am half-dressed and looking for my car keys before I have properly woken up and feel a familiar ache, like hunger.

It's been fifteen years. My husband and I are renting a tiny house in Glasthule. He has hooked himself up to his office in London; he works till three every afternoon, while I walk in loops around the neighbourhood, reacquainting myself with it. In the evening, we go swimming at the Forty Foot with red faced, whiskery men, they are like friendly lobsters.

What surprises me is all that has not changed. The line of the seafront and a certain green light that comes into the sky when there is sun after rain and the way I feel when I see it, scared and happy both. The whistled Irish 'T'. *Whattt's thattt?* The man in the train station who pretends not to remember me then winks and charges me schoolgirl fare, for larks.

My old self has been here all along and the seam of fifteen years is an invisible one. It feels like a revelation. 'All travel is a kind of time travel,' I try to explain to my husband, but it turns out he knew this already, it is a proven scientific theory.

We visit Lily, my old schoolfriend. Lily and I share little but the dogged loyalty that is essential to any friendship. 'She wrote to me every week for a year when mother died,' I whisper as we ring the doorbell. My spirits still lift every time I see Lily's large, friendly handwriting.

Twenty years ago Lily chose me for her friend. 'You are my kind of person,' she told me, three hours after she'd joined our school, brash, confident, already having cheeked her first teacher. The next day: 'You shouldn't try to talk to boys,' she said, sitting on the teacher's desk at lunchtime, swinging her legs. 'I've seen you. You're a disaster. You blush. What you should do is stay quiet and just look at them.' Within a week, 'with your looks,' she told me confidentially in the girls' loos, teaching me how to put on eyeliner, 'and my personality, you could get any guy you wanted.' Wrong on both counts, I thought, but I was flattered anyway. She came over after school. We ate plums in the back garden.

Afterwards Lily said: 'Your mother's very sweet. That plait – she's such a hippy. Did she ever think of dyeing her hair?'

My mother said: 'Lily's very sweet. She reminds me of an over-grown puppy.'

Lily said: 'Your mother's very brave to bring you up alone.'

I said: 'It's not like she's got a choice.'

Lily said: 'She could always marry again. You need a father figure.'

My mother and I are sitting at the kitchen table in Sandycove. We have just come home from the shops with a bag of hard kiwi fruit, the first either of us have ever seen. My mother slices one open and gazes at it, then holds one cut half up to me. An imperfect kaleidoscope, rays fanning out to the hairy edges, an abundance of tiny black seeds nestling in the radiant green. 'When I look at this I think I can believe in God,' my mother says. Her eyes are shining. Afterwards we eat the kiwi fruit and make faces at each other, it's so beautiful, but bitter.

Lily hugs us and shouts for her husband and they bustle around getting drinks for us. She is pregnant now, and her husband has a matching pot belly. They are like two skittles.

My husband is ill at ease. I can tell by the hearty way he is admiring everything.

Lily takes us upstairs to show us the baby's room. All ready with two months to go. She can't help planning ahead. A mobile throws shadows on the wall, there is the smell of paint and there is something dark and alive in the cot – it is Lily's large, ancient cat. I knew him as a kitten. We watch his fur rise and fall as he sleeps, a slight growl in his breathing.

'Enjoy it while you can, sunshine. You'll be out on your ear soon enough,' Lily tells him.

'We'll take him,' my husband jokes. 'Don't throw him out on the street.'

'Oh, that's not what I meant at all,' Lily says and my husband says, 'Oh, I know you didn't –'

I think, the evening will be full of these tiny misunderstandings.

My mother and Harold met in the Ritz. We used to tell people this and wait carefully before supplying the second piece of information: the Ritz is a chip shop in Dun Laoghaire. The mailboat was late and when Harold got to his hotel the kitchen was closed. It was a Sunday night. There was nowhere else to go. But when it came to paying he realised he had no Irish money. My mother was in the queue. 'Let me get that,' my mother said and that was that; they had to arrange to meet again so Harold, terribly embarrassed to be caught without funds, could repay her.

Ironic, given what followed.

She got back into the car and I asked: 'What kept you?' And she smiled and said: 'Bit of a queue.' Our chips were nearly cold.

The next day, after school, there were Harold and my mother having tea under the plum tree. Harold stood up, beaming, blinking in the sun and said: '*Look at you!* I've been hearing all about you. I want to hear everything that happened you today.' I liked Harold. 'I feel like I've come home,' Harold said, much later that evening, as the shadows crept along the grass.

They still have not settled on a name for the baby. 'Holly for a girl, Jack for a boy,' Lily's husband says when we are sitting down. 'Keep it simple.'

Lily says: 'This is what he keeps saying. But those names are too popular.'

'Lily wants our kid to stand out from the crowd, I think little *Tarquin* or *Zebedee* may have other views when he's old enough to express them, God help him.'

'All I've said,' Lily says placidly, 'is if it's a girl I want Isabelle. With an L-E.'

My husband clears his throat. 'They say there are three sentences you should try out when choosing a name,' he says, 'and I think Isabelle is fine for all of them. But just to make the point, let me demonstrate with a more exotic name. Say Fluffy.'

Lily is frowning, she thinks he is mocking her.

'You should try saying: one, "I love you, Fluffy." Two, "Can Fluffy come out to play?" And three, "We are considering Fluffy for promotion."'

Everybody laughs but Lily. 'I like Isabelle,' she says stubbornly. 'Your mother was Isabel,' she says to me, as though I have forgotten. 'No L-E,' I smile. 'Not that posh.'

'She was posh, though,' Lily says. 'But not snobby,' she adds hastily. 'Just a wonderful woman. Such a shame,' she says to my husband, 'you never knew her. Tragic. But she's alive as long as we remember her. Let's drink to her.' I am mortified but glad too, Lily is the only person who will ever do this.

Harold's apartment in London smelled like an airport. My mother said, we are only here till Harold's work settles down. Fifty minutes away by plane! We can come home every weekend if we want. But in the meantime Harold said we should rent out the Sandycove house, for what he called cashflow.

My mother stopped cooking, because Harold liked to eat out. I discovered a sweet powdery almond ice cream called kulfi in a Lebanese restaurant. 'Harold,' I said, 'let's come here every night.' Harold would do anything for me as long as I was enthusiastic and so I did eat kulfi every night for a month, and they started ordering a second bottle of wine most nights, which made Harold confused and clownish. Clutching my mother's knees in the taxi home his glasses rakish falling off his ear Harold was adorable, you could see why my mother packed up the house followed Harold to London would follow him anywhere.

My mother stopped mending my clothes, because Harold said the sight of the sewing basket made him think of the penury of his youth. 'Hit the shops,' Harold said gaily, unrolling a wad of banknotes on which the severe Queen pursed her lips at excessive expenditure. 'Live a little!' We went to Harvey Nichols. We spent a sinful amount of money on a tailored jacket and skirt for me all threaded with gold. We were jokey and elated as we bought it but I was snappy on the way home, then she was, then she fell silent altogether. 'It's wrong, wrong, wrong, to spend all that money on a suit for a spoiled little girl,' was all she would say in the end, and I never wore it.

My mother abandoned gardening, she had to, except for pots. She filled Harold's balcony with geraniums, because geraniums would grow anywhere my mother said, geraniums would grow in the palm of your hand. When you shredded a geranium leaf the lemon smell was Sandycove and our old kitchen windowsill.

My mother is the pink valerian in an old granite wall and the clink of the milk bottle on the porch in Sandycove. She is *get* not *fetch* and *I will* not *I shall* and *I was sitting* not *I was sat*. Harold is *chop chop* and *live a little* and *oh good grief* and *wh-wh-wh-what's the matter now?* Harold was teased in school for his stammer, 'teased,' he says, the language of the older generation. Bullied, more like. Harold's lower lip quivers when he is cross with you. Harold is funny when he is cross and I tell him this.

'Funny peculiar or funny ha ha?' The word peculiar makes me think of peculiar smells, cheese and socks, and Harold too, and I laugh. 'That kind of funny, I see,' Harold says coldly and I can see he is going to sulk for the day. I can't bear it when Harold sulks but my mother has a kind of long-distance ability to shut out Harold's black moods for as long as it takes for Harold to crack and go to her, where she sits queen-like, calmly sipping tea, and listens to him beg her forgiveness.

'And what else?' my husband asks both me and Lily, the door is open now.

Harold got a stroke then it was two years of specialists and Harold still no better. The bills were astronomical. My mother gritted her teeth and said: 'We'll have to sell Sandycove.' But Harold told her (clutching his head, from pain, or guilt) he had already sold it. My mother did not react. 'Well, where are the proceeds? It's crazy, all these bills.' It was far too complicated, Harold said, he would sort it out as soon as he got back on his feet, but that did not happen, instead he had a second stroke, and the complications began with paying for the funeral, which was a far less elaborate affair than Harold might have wished for.

My mother spent two years trying to settle his debts and not to blame him and mourning him and yearning for home and through all this I was no comfort to her. I know because she told me so once, though I have tried to forget that she ever said so.

'It was the stress talking. The stress was what killed her in the end,' Lily says comfortingly, as though she knows anything about it, but I am grateful to her anyway.

Things finish early. We come home and open a bottle of wine and I find I want to propose a toast to Harold. I miss him too.

Later, my husband starts to make sandwiches.

'Wouldn't that make you believe in God?' I challenge him, picking up an avocado half to show him.

The creamy yellow-green is like thick paint.

'Well, it's certainly beautiful,' he says. He takes it in his hand, he smells it, he feels the pale egg-shaped hollow where the stone was. He slides a finger under the ripe reptilian skin and nudges it off in one floppy piece. He lays the half-avocado flat side down on the chopping board.

'To everything its time,' he says firmly, regretfully. The knife goes through it like butter.

Poems

MARK LAWLOR

Thursday

Seven herons rise
touch burnt springs
in the calendar of fire –

St John's night;
whose blaze
burns the furthest?

One gets to the lake,
hisses in water,
field of rust wheels

swans ignore.
They sow feathers
through bog fields;

a heron utters
like a picked scab.

Yellow

Bastard saffron fuels the lamp,
ablaze orange-yellow to greet you.
The room quickens with gifts

jealous *fleur-de-lis* counter-poise,
fingers of an outstretched hand.
Gravely its perfume opens –

it burns him out of his element,
frog scissors to his palm,
she needs love, not scald.

Hand stings in the irised pond.
Her weirdness becomes natural,
uncurls his hand and drips;

a laburnum so close to the house
opens the eye —

Honey

Eyes stare through the shelter of trees in wonderment.
Christ has left his jacket hung on a branch. Its wings burst
to ochre tears. A boy shivers, a tear stings him on the lips,
gives birth to song, opens a curtain into an amber room.
Queen, on a throne of bees, waxes her mouth, gathers bees,
tastes them. They all have duty. Spits out afresh and afresh.

Hare

Over sticks he leaps to a blood pattern
clear as a harebell puddle of now,
his meuse lands him in trouble,
cries of men haunt trees at dusk.

He kindles evening's breath,
crouches, lugs flat and wise,
no thoughts of decay in his form,
light brown iris never rests

in the map lit by up-country moon.
He's a pet lamp of rushy fields,
all inhale as he breaks cover,
haunch shoots into what he is.

Uproar then at nightfall,
he knows that haemorrhage is rain.

2 Proposals

FRANCES BYRNES

Mr Redfern lives at number 151. By the time you get that far up our road the houses are detached. He's got savannah grasses in his front garden, which is a bit outré given his age. He says the doctor told him he'll make it to 100.

Ada, his wife, did before she died last year in a cold snap. Her last words to him were, 'Walter! Straighten your spine!'

He was planting bulbs with a hat on when I arrived. He invited me to sit down with him in his hut, laying his hat on the pile of logs he's chopped for the winter.

'Oh dear. Huts,' he said.

He lifted a finger, and we listened to a wood pigeon.

'My sister died in a hut, tha knows?'

'I didn't know you had a sister.'

'She had the consumption when she were a child, and so our step-father who hadn't taken to us put her out to live in the garden hut, day and night. He had me make her meals and take 'em out to her. Until, one day, that were that.'

'I'm sorry.'

'We'd nowt to our name, were orphans, you see. And when I look back, I can't fathom it; someone well-to-do like Ada having someone like me. Her having been to the convent. Not that she wa' papist. But they sent her to the Catholics because she wa' delicate.'

'Well, the nuns must have done something for her, if she survived to 103!'

'No, that wa' because she was a 7. Which brings me to why you're here.'

He took his gardening gloves off and faced me.

'Ada told me, "Walter, after I'm gone – and I will be afore long — you'll want to get thee-self wed again and you could do worse than that Ellen. Ellen, from 1-0-2. She is a 9". That's Ada talking. As you know, I don't take heed of the numerology but Ada swore by it.'

I was astounded. I said, to be certain, 'Are you proposing to me, Mr Redfern?' There was a taste in my mouth, which was like tea with just-gone-off milk in it.

'I am,' he said. 'I'm not much for the how's-your-father, I must say. But I have me ways and they're not all bad. I am 95 you know.'

I hadn't seen it coming. 'Didn't you say you had some Quality Street for me to take back down for Mum?' I asked.

'How is your mother? How's the hip?'

'Well, she's not galloping yet, but she's coming along.'

'How are you around the house?'

'Pardon, Mr Redfern?'

'Tha knows what I mean.'

'Well, I like washing up but not putting away.' I played along for time, flabbergasted. 'I'm not a great one for cooking. Unless you like frozen-pea soup. You might get some mint in it, on a good day.'

'Well, her at 166 can bring that stew.'

'Her at 166' had once taken the Redferns some chicken chasseur when I was up visiting. Ada had said to her, 'Have you brought us some more of that horrible stew? Because we don't like it. What do you do to it? Do you put too much pepper in it or what?' Mrs 166 had backed out still wearing her mac and holding her pot, looking winded.

I said, 'I wouldn't be too sure about that.'

'I know. I lived with Ada for 70 years, and found her quite frank for most of them. She did teach me how to make Parkin, though.'

The wind picked up through the trees behind us.

'Summat's brewing out there,' said Walter. 'You know, Ada and I lived through the worst two storms of the century.' He loosened his gardening tie, then recalled there was a lady present and tightened it again.

'During the Sheffield storm of 1920 summat we were living next door but one to each other but we didn't know it. We weren't fated to meet, actually, until Ada moved with her parents to help run a boarding house in Blackpool.'

'That's an unusual colour to paint your guttering,' I nodded up to his aquamarine drains, wondering how not to hurt him.

'Go and have a look inside,' he said. So, feeling ridiculous, almost in peril, I did. I walked in through the original 1950s kitchen. It looked cleaner than Ada kept it. She had sticky dirt on all her surfaces, including her clothes. The sitting room smelled of lingering gas, as usual. I picked a bric-a-brac vase off the mantelpiece, and underneath it was a scrap of paper with a name on. I gingerly lifted a china dog: another name. One of the names was my mother's. Ada had once said to her: "Pick a vase or something and put your name to it, and we might let you have it after we've gone." I set a pan of water to heat on his stove and went back outside.

'In the second worst storm of the century,' he said, back at his spade, turning the soil, 'It were 1950 summat. We were driving the Bentley through the Vale of Evesham when the sky started lowering. I could see it coming from the West. Ada was whinnying, because she hated thunder. The storm caught up with us where the apple trees are. I pulled over to take shelter, but Ada wouldn't budge out of the car seat. So I says, put your head down and I'll cover you o'er with a blanket, which is what happened, her 'ead between her legs, and she kept calling, "Not yet Lord!" and weeping, "I'm not ready to meet me maker."'

Walter's eyes filled.

'But latterly, she were ready for Him. After the heart attack the doctor said, 'It's 50/50 for her now, Mr Redfern.' Well, the 50/50 were facing the wrong way. I'm not grumbling. I've got to abide by it. Her time had come.'

I listened again to the story of Ada's last night. A little after midnight Ada had called out, "Who's going to look after my Walter?" When she'd been answered with a polite, "We are," by two of Walter's work acquaintances, kind, decent sorts down from Durham, Ada had said, "Oh," very nonplussed.

'And then she died. Well, you go when your number's up, was her thing.'

The couple have been very good at stocking up his freezer, and driving down from Durham when his computer crashes.

'I have kept my accounts very properly, you know,' he told me. 'So if I were to go, they'd all be in order. I was hired for my handwriting.'

He was a clerk, a scribe. I imagined him at a high desk, with blotting paper and an inkwell.

'You're three times my age, Mr Redfern.'

'Am I?'

I thought, what about the nights? On sheets that would feel solid as old wallpaper? The Christmas presents they'd unearthed for us from the back of their wardrobe hadn't been savoury: a mothballed nightdress, a pair of socks with a used sticking plaster in one of them, violet lozenges with no sell-by date. But, then, I am a fettler. And I let myself wonder. It would be an experience.

'So, Ellen?' asked Walter.

I could smell the smoky foliage in the high trees behind us. The earth on his trowel.

'You ruminate while I mash the tea.'

I looked at the large house. The leaded lights, four bedrooms, wondering if he'd accept conditions. How long he would live for. Perhaps I might actually like making sponge cake and frying liver. I watched as a woman of about 80, emerging from her French windows next door, directed her gardener back to the gate at the far end of her garden. She looked astonished to see Walter had a visitor. Her gardener made an awkward about-turn with the wheelbarrow of autumn mulch which he'd gleaned from under her privet, and he headed off towards the woods.

'She's a good-looking woman, for her age,' said Walter, conspiratorially, creeping up on me with the teapot. 'And mind, I have thought about it. But how could you live with someone who polishes her drive with a duster?'

I laughed, and our eyes met. We brought the deck chairs out of the hut. He forced his Parkin on me, which was rock hard. It splintered in my mouth.

'Yes well. There's only the Insurance to get your name on, if you'll have me. I called 'em today to get a form sent out, but it wa' the electronic lady and I couldn't make head ner tail of it.'

'You old romantic,' I chided.

'I'm not.'

'How did you propose to Ada?'

'I proposed to Ada on my fourth stay at her parents' lodging house in Blackpool.'

'Did you go on your holidays there alone?'

'I did. I took me sen off to Blackpool every Christmas. Well, I'd no one. And that's how I met her. After three Christmases they all knew I were going to ask her to marry me, but I took me time. On the fourth year I took a ring wi' me, and I put it out on breakfast table on the Boxing Day. When she came to take the orders I said, you know, pointing it out to her, "Do you want it?"'

I laughed. But he was being serious. *Do you want it.*

'And she warn't that impressed wi' t' ring. She couldn't help but speak plainly. She said, "Well, it's not what I'd 'ave chosen meself, but alright then."'

I shook my head, with a smile.

A dog raced along the woodland path, panting. It alerted birds that scattered from under a holly bush. Walter and I turned to watch. A squirrel, two blackbirds.

'Have you taken into account, Ellen, the virtue of having woods at the end of your garden? Given that your mother's house just has that little patch of grass behind, and whatever's backing onto it, being as you're on the even side of the road. We have foxes here, on the odd numbers. And you know the bluebells tek over in May. At night you can hear water in stream. And the trees are right beautiful.'

'Yes. I love the woods.'

The berries and the curling bracken. It would be lovely to be able to disappear always out of the back of the house, and straight into the trees.

So I looked to the woods, the burnt toffee autumn in them, touching the sky up above us, every year growing higher and deeper.

'Walter what happens to trees? Do they just keep on growing? Or stop at a particular height? Do they die at a certain age? And then what? I wonder what happens to trees.'

Authors

Trudy Hayes's short stories have been widely published. Her play *Out Of My Head* was nominated for the Stewart Parker Theatre award; *Making Love To Yorick* was performed in the Dublin and Belfast Fringe Theatre festivals. She has published a pamphlet, *The Politics of Seduction* and her work is included in *Ireland's Women's Writings Past and Present* and other anthologies.

Robert Monroe has studied at Harvard and Trinity, and has worked in fiction, poetry, music and film. He is working on a novel.

Noel Conneely lives in Dublin and has had poems published in *Cyphers, Poetry Ireland Review, The Shop*, and *Willow Review*.

Ruth Greenberg was born in London in 1979. She studied English Literature at Trinity College and is now writing a feature length screenplay.

Jacqueline McCarrick grew up in London and Ireland. She studied Performing Arts at Middlesex University, the Lee Strasberg Academy, and the Actors Studio in New York. She has directed numerous productions including a cross-border *Romeo and Juliet*, Berkoff's *Lunch* at Andrews Lane, *Henry V*, and Beckett's *Quad*. She has had two staged readings at the Old Vic, *The Mushroom Pickers* and *The Moth Hour*. She is currently working on the third of this trilogy, as well as two new pieces.

Peter Sheridan was born and reared in Dublin, graduated in Galway and is currently living in Mountjoy Square. He writes avidly and also attempts making music.

Jeannette Pascoe was born in Houston, Texas, graduated in English from Trinity University in San Antonio, and is now living in Louisville, Kentucky where she is writing a collection of stories and a play.

Karen Bender worked as a freelance writer and script consultant before coming to Dublin. She has received National Endowment and New York Foundation of the Arts awards in support of her writing.

Alex Mavor was born in 1981 and grew up in Scotland. Having graduated from Oxford last year he now lives in Musselburgh. He is working on two collections: one poetry, one short stories.

Dudley Cruse was born in Nelspruit, South Africa in 1981. He completed his undergraduate studies in 2002 receiving a BSc in Biodiversity and Ecology.

Catriona Mitchell was born in Switzerland and raised in Scotland and Australia. She has lived in Ireland for five years. She is writing a novel set in Germany, for which she recently received a research grant from the Arts Council.

Sarah Binchy grew up in Dublin where she works as a print journalist and radio and television producer.

Mark Lawlor is from Cavan. He received a BA in Drama and Theatre Studies from Trinity College and is working on a collection of poetry.

Frances Byrnes produces radio programmes for BBC Radio 3 and 4, working mostly with writers and dancers. She is working on a novel.